ISBN-10: 1478273194

ISBN-13: 9781478273196

Dedicated to all the dog lovers out there

In Memoriam of Kathleen Lacey Henne,
a sorority friend who loved dogs, fostered and advocated
for homeless dogs through her HART group (Homeless Animals
Rescue Team), and would have been amused by Della's
mischievous adventures.

ACKNOWLEDGEMENTS

First of all, I would like to thank Mark Zuckerberg for inventing such a great social networking website and without Facebook this book would not have happened.

I cannot express enough gratitude for my Facebook friends for their interesting comments and countless likes as well as tremendous support for Della. And it has been enlightening to hear these friends' stories and experiences about their own pets as well as helpful suggestions on how to resolve a puppy issue such as eating a lipstick. In fact, Facebook is a good learning tool. Without those comments, I would have never thought of publishing this book. Thank you, my dear friends, for being a part of the team!

Jana Underwood, who owns a boarding and daycare facility Happy Tails, has done an excellent job with her photography as there are many amazing images of Della in this book. Whenever you see "Happy Tails" in any post with a photo, then you know who took that picture. Thank you, Jana, for the awesome still shots of Della and her friends romping around at your daycare. And thanks to the Happy Tails staff – Jesse, Gwen, Cliff, Kirk, Yvette, Cindy, and Jackie - for putting up with Della's mischievous actions such as unlocking the gate in the indoor pen and opening every door to the lobby - and taking the blame from their boss Jana before the final capture of the "Houdini Dog".

Whenever you need a good dog trainer, Lisa Rapacki is the one. She managed to teach Della to "Sit! Down! Stay!" whenever offering a treat.

That would make Della look like a Greek Sphinx. Thanks, Lisa, for making this wild, crazy puppy a bit more manageable.

Friendship Veterinary Hospital has patiently tolerated Della's not-so-dire emergency visits despite its busy schedules and I would like to thank its staff for fixing up Della such as reducing her bee-stung face with antibiotics. And I am sure that the Friendship veterinarians and staffers will keep Della out of trouble for many years to come. Well, maybe they should keep an hour open for Della everyday just in case of emergency...

Finally, I thank my husband Steve for the best birthday present ever: Della. I appreciate him for believing that a 50-year-old is never too old for a rambunctious puppy. And thank you, Nora Morioni-Holm, for breeding such a great Lab litter and prodding Steve to buy Della.

And one more time...Thank you, Della, for being a great puppy, albeit your mischief. You have brought a great deal of love and laughter into our household. We love you, Della!

Prologue

My almost daily postings about Della on Facebook began on my 50th birthday when my husband Steve surprised me with this tiny little seven-week-old yellow Lab, her neck adorned with a giant red bow. We had discussed getting a puppy four years after our beloved Lab Olive passed away, even drinking her last glass of Cabernet Sauvignon an hour before we put her down due to an age-related ailment. But then we had Mabel the mutt who was about to turn fifteen, too old to run around and play despite her good health; therefore, we decided to drop the idea of a puppy for the time being. We felt that Mabel deserved peace and quiet during the remaining part of her life.

But Steve changed his mind after his co-worker Nora announced a litter of Lab puppies at her farm in Gloucester, a seaside town in Southeastern Virginia. So he went out there and picked Della for her huge feet, remembering our deceased Olive's love for swimming. Four days later he presented Della to me at my birthday party and I was shell-shocked but thrilled with a new addition to our childless family. Mabel our other dog apparently had forgotten how to play due to her age and slept most of the time, steering clear of the puppy - until the last few months of her life.

Thus began Facebook postings on Della. The idea of this book "Della on Facebook" popped up three months later when I realized how much my friends love hearing Della's adventures according to their comments, many of which are humorous and creative. Some of these comments regale with my friends' own canine experiences; other comments offer great suggestions such as what to do when your dog eats a beer can. For this book I am selecting only some, not all of the comments, for each posting since many comments have similar sayings. You would not want to read 40 comments that say "Awww, cute" below one post. The selected comments have not been edited for this book because in my opinion they should be left as they are so the readers will get a true sense of Facebook. And to protect their privacy, I will not disclose my friends' names except for a few first names that deserve a reply or play a big role in Della's life.

In all, everyone is pretty much writing this book!

July 16, 2011

Look what I got for my birthday!

(Minute-long video of Della wandering on our brick patio, then walking up to Bainy, sniffing her recording cell phone, and finally being picked up by Steve)

36 Likes, 54 Comments

------*Beautiful Puppy. Happy Birthday!*

------*Oh I think I'm in love. What a wonderful birthday present.*

------*Awwww!! So wicked cute!*

------*Pretty Pup! Huge feet...lanky and loveable. A reminder of our Nuthin when he was a baby (10 years old now)*

------*LIKE LIKE LIKE LIKE LIKE LIKE LIKE!!!!! Best present ever!!!*

------*I want one for my bd!*

------*The gift that keeps on giving!* ☺

------*(From Della's breeder Nora) It was very hard not being able to post anything about the pup since we wanted you to be surprised. I am so happy you have her, Della. I know you will be pleased. Steve was excited, too. We still have 8 pups left. Pass the word! Happy Birthday, Bainy!*

July 16 (Second post, later in the afternoon)

Della's nap after her first wading in our fishpond. Next will be the ocean. Definitely a swimmer already.

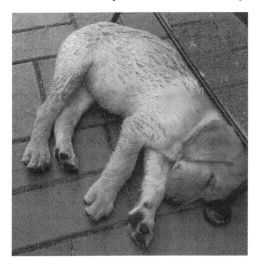

38 Likes, 29 Comments

------*Plum tuckered out...*

------*Super Cute and with those big webbed paws, she will be an excellent swimmer!*

------*My girls can't wait to meet her!*

------*OMG, she is PRECIOUS!!*

------WOW, I miss having a puppy...too cute..love the pic and got to love water babies!!! Fort Boykin near Carrolton/Smithfield is really nice for learning to swim pre-ocean. It is the James River, but shallow and no waves.

------Get sleep now so can stay up all night!!! Lol

------You got a puppy!!! I know you and Steve are dog lovers!! we do still have dogs...One big one, and two little ones... we love them!!

------PUPPY LOVE

------Are you going to train her as a hearing dog?

July 17

You should know something about a puppy: Don't go spending all the money on the best squeaky or indestructible toys you can ever find because a puppy usually goes berserk with an empty plastic soda bottle. All you have to do is throw that bottle across the kitchen floor and the puppy will attack it. You know how much noise a plastic bottle makes when hitting the walls...

3 Likes, 9 Comments

------(From Nora the breeder)They love old socks that are tied in knots, too. Bailey, her mommie, loved plastic bottles when she was little. Now she likes squeaky toys.

------You're so right, Bainy! Kinda like little kids with pots and pans.

------(Bainy comments) It was amazing tonight when Della placed all of her toys including the tied old socks into her crate. What a smart dog – we just love Della to death!

------paper towel rolls are also a big hit!

------my girls prefer the toys they steal from other dogs to the ones I actually buy

------Yeah Stephanie, If I am not watching Skyler (my lab) while walking she picks up other dogs toys and children's ball. One time she carried a ball to a croquet set a block before I noticed.

July 18

Good Afternoon.

35 Likes, 40 Comments

------Will be a Giant? Big Paws! ;)

------So cute pup!!! what is your pup's name?

------(Bainy replies) Della, after Steve's out-in-the-boonies grandmother

------I think Lab puppies and Golden puppies corner the market on cute!

------*she poses like a model* ☺

------*beware of a waaaayyyy tooooooo cute puppy. mischief lurks behind those soft eyes.....*

------*bainy, I want one! Are there any left?*

------*Welcome to the neighborhood, Della!*

------*I think she's ready for a pawdicure*

------*Let's send this adorable puppy to straighten out the Rupert Murdoch mess*

July 19

With a 7-week-old puppy, I feel like a mother with sextuplets.

6 Likes, 1 Comment

------*Hope you aren't nursing!*

July 20

Just took Della to see my folks at Harbor's Edge and had the puppy play in the courtyard. Since Dad has been through so much healthwise, it was the first time in five years I'd seen him smile that big when Della lapped up his face. Mom said she and Dad thoroughly enjoyed a visit from their new "granddog."

38 Likes, 13 Comments

------*that is wonderful!*

------*Bainy I read your post to my mom at lunch today and showed her pictures of the puppy. She said to tell you SHE wouldn't like the licking but it made her laugh! So fun to see her laugh! And as soon as I said your* name she smiled and said Oh! Bainy! Dementia is cruel but the past is her refuge and joy.

------(Bainy replies) Cathy, please give your mother my love.

------Animals know how to give the special love. So glad your Dad was able to enjoy the "granddog!!!!!"

------I am sure it was a treat for everyone there!!!!!

------You hear so much about therapy dogs for the elderly doing wonders! I'm sure they will have a regular visitor now.

------Della could be one of those hospital visiting dogs. Glad to hear it made your dad smile. 8-)

July 20

Help! How can I distract my puppy from my shoelaces while I'm walking???

4 Likes, 19 Comments

------spray water at her when she attacks you!! ☺

------Velcro straps...

------Tuck the laces in while around the puppy. ☺

------Give her a chew toy. As many times as it takes

------Sprinkle some hot pepper on them.

------bitter apple!

------wear flip flops??

------Get another shoelace and hold it in front of her while she walks???

------Velcro closure shoes.

------call dog whisperer

------ttsshhtt...along with a "bite" from the fingers. You know, Cesar style!

July 21

There is an advantage of owning a periodically hyper puppy: I've lost a pound.

5 Likes, 0 Comments

July 21

Paper Towel Roll: Thank you for distracting my puppy from my shoelaces.

8 Likes, 3 Comments

------Kong toy – fill it with peanut butter and freeze – guaranteed to keep the puppy occupied, though it does get messy.

------that's a glass half full attitude there, Bainy!

------I feel for ya Bainy. We're almost past that stage with Bear, although most everything he gets hold of gets shredded. And he will be three in August.

July 23

Moment of silence for my pretty red petunia that had been yanked out of its little wheelbarrow flowerpot by the puppy...

6 Likes, 8 Comments

------*takes off imaginary hat, puts it to her chest, and lowers her head*

------We need your puppy to meet our puppy!

------When you have a puppy, nothing is sacred any more, shoes, plants, furniture, nothing! Hide anything you want to keep, lol

------(From Nora the breeder)You are still calling her the puppy, not the devil. That is a good sign. Thank you for referring Matt Myrick to me. He bought one of Della's sisters. He will be back in the morning at 9am to pick her up.

------That means I need a moment of silence for just about everything in my backyard....NEKO! >☹

------awww....

------Poor little petunia!! Bad pup

------and it's only the beginning heeheehee

July 24

Never wear a knee-length floppy skirt around a puppy or you'll face an embarrassing situation.

9 Likes, 1 Comment

------LOL

July 25

Now playing on this computer with Della on the floor chewing my shoelaces. Why not let her? I've got enough punctures on my arms and ankles from puppy bites. Geez, those teeth are as sharp as a bowl of sewing needles.

1 Like, 5 Comments

------Buy her her very own pair of sneakers (Dollar store) with laces

------(Bainy replies) Connie, are you crazy? If I buy Della her own shoes, then she'll develop a very bad habit and turn to OUR shoes!

------I agree with you on that point Bainy! WOW. Develop the good habits – Dentley's beef knuckles are great chew-targets and a far better item than shoes. LOL They don't splinter like some of the other chew bones. We should get together for a doggie play date soon. Sasha LOVES puppies.

------(Embarrassed Connie replies to Bainy's appalled comment) Good point... it's the heat lol

------better get her chewing on the right things....we have the experience of 2 labs to know this fact...

July 26

Dog-tired Della

28 Likes, 24 Comments

------*Those are some BIG puppy feet!!!*

------*she's doubled in size!*

------*So sweet and almost human.*

------*too cute and some big puppy feet...she's going to be BIG!!*

------*Somebody needs to paint this as a portrait, wow!*

------*Lounging on the bed. So spoiled!*

------lucky spoil rotten puppy ☺ thou she deserves it just like any other pampered dogs, right? ☺ Not their fault just because they're not human beings but dogs! Lol I love that name Della!

------What is in that dog food? All the love must be growing her!!

July 27

Unbelievable. Della at 15 inches tall wanted to play with a neighbor's gigantic wolfhound. She's indeed a social dog.

8 Likes, 3 Comments

------lol...those dogs are Ginormous!

------(From Nora the breeder) Bainy, Nessa one of our CRNAs just got Della's sister. She describes her just as you describe Della. Taking her toys to the crate. We have two black males left! ;-)

------She has a "social momma!" ☺

July 29

Day 13 with a 9-week-old puppy: Two inches taller; flattened hostas and liriope; numerous trash bags of newspapers; increased kitchen activity; constant noise of high-tech squeaky toys; licks taking over bites; delayed human aging; growing love; and miraculously no shredded shoes so far!

25 Likes; 5 Comments

------New life phase for sure!

------sounds like me last summer with Hutch! It's amazing how fast they grow!

------the shoes, the coats, and lampshades come at 6 months!

------that your puppy quite cool smile

------lol

July 29

WTH? Della in her strange sleeping position...

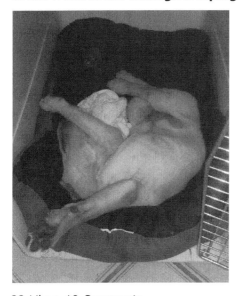

22 Likes, 19 Comments

------I LOVE a dog with personality. It looks like you got one!

------They say people who sleep flayed out that feel very secure...

------Definitely a secure pup!

------Has she done the "superman" pose yet?

------That looks like a Doga asana.

------HAHA..is that a Yoga pose, Connie?

------I wish I could sleep like that....not a care in the world!

------LOL looks like one dog leg and the rest is chicken. Body and wings. I just cannot see the dog's head.....oh by the way I have vision problem!!!!

------You should cherish your puppy's funny sleeping positions. Puppies tend to do that. I miss my doggies' funny sleeping positions when they were puppies.

------a little scary til you expand the image

July 30

Della's first swim lesson at Happy Tails

(Short video of Lisa Rapacki the dog trainer encouraging Della to swim in the small pool at Happy Tails, a doggie daycare in Norfolk, and then a pooped-out Della at home)

18 Likes, 14 Comments

------I love it! Maybe Dock Dogs will be next?

------Her feet are HUGE!!!!

------I didn't realize dogs had to have swimming lessons

------Actually from what they told me, it's not instinctive. Dogs can drown...this new facility is wonderful. They do a great job grooming and also have daycare!!! LOVE HAPPY TAILS!!

July 31

I like an overcast Sunday for a change of pace. No guilt about being cooped up in the house to clean up the puppy's mess as well as ours.

7 Likes, 2 Comments

------Della still making messes?

------pouring rain is for that too...lol

August 2

Uh oh. A female osprey has been flying around my yard surrounded by pine trees in the past few days. Some of the fish in my ponds have become dinner. That's why I don't buy those pricey kois.

1 Like, 9 Comments

------(From Nora the breeder) Look out for Della, too! They will prey on her as well.

------(Bainy replies) I know...I don't let her out of my sight. Della's getting bigger everyday so that helps.

------(Nora replies) All of the pups are gone. They were beautiful litter. They all went to very special homes. I am so glad you got the beauty of the litter.

------Bainy, ospreys eat fish...they are "fish eagles" They don't eat dogs – especially Della size dogs! They may "attack" anything that gets too close to their nest if there is a nest nearby. Otherwise, your pup has no worries in regard to the Osprey!

------200-dollar koi dinners are not cool. Safe places are.

August 2

Della was eating her supper when the house phone rang at 6:30 PM and looked up in puzzlement. I tell you, I can't wait until she gets big enough to growl at phone solicitors.

5 Likes, 0 Comments

August 3

Della gets her mouth on anything including our little garden Gargoyle. She thinks she can eat concrete. The Gargoyle wins.

5 Likes, 3 Comments

------She needed more minerals in her diet???

------she was just sharpening her teeth for all other objects ☺

------Hey Bainy, I have a two year old that still chews everything he can get his mouth on and I cannot let him loose outside or he will chase the horses and get kicked in the head or take off after something in the woods. He has already dug up a couple of moles!

August 4

Took Della to the beach for the first time and she had the biggest time of her life. The ocean was a little rough but Della had a chance to wade in the 8"deep sandbar puddle. Flirted with people including toddlers and rolled around on the cool dune under my parents' cottage. She thought sand was gold. I see why kids had sandboxes in the early days.

10 Likes, 1 Comment

------(From Nora the breeder) Nessa got one of Della's sisters. See her picture of Phoebe at the beach swimming in the waves. ;-)

August 6

Following the dog trainer's advice, we made a "shake can" for Della to quiet her whining whenever she is put in her comfy grate at night or for a nap. It's a Coke can with 20 pennies inside and works like a miracle. Steve jokingly said he would use that can to stop my talking or asking too many questions. Very funny...

12 Likes, 0 Comments

August 7

A $12 plastic wading pool from Kmart is a godsend for Della during this heat of summer – before she gets big and transfers to an actual swimming pool at Happy Tails.

9 Likes, 2 Comments

------(From Jana the owner of Happy Tails) YAY! We are so ready for Della! ☺

------Great idea!

August 8

There's nothing wrong with your back legs, Della

(42-second Video of Della refusing to get up when playing tug-of-war with a towel pulled by Bainy. She just dragged her legs for a good 200 feet across the grassy yard as if she was paralyzed from the waist down. After being urged to get up by Bainy's annoyed voice, Della finally did in the end and chased the towel)

8 Likes, 23 Comments

------I think she was practicing her breast stroke...back to Happy Tails to let her show off.

------She's got you wrapped around her little dewclaw!

------Too funny. Guess the brain has not told the back legs to move yet.

------Maybe Della can teach a few of our Happy Tails Dogs that trick.

------It's so sweet to see you take your dog for a drag!

------You may have to bleach that cute tummy...

------Awww! It's nice of you and Steve to grow that plush green carpet for her to slide around on!

------I think she's part snake!

August 9

Don't you love when you worry over something and your husband says it won't happen and then it DOES happen? During my three-hour absence Della got loose in the house after managing to push up a gate hook in the kitchen and damaged my only dried grass arrangement. Came home to find it strewn all over the living room and poor Mabel with a I-didn't-do-it look. Well, I went out and bought new SAFETY hooks as I'd earlier suggested. I knew it, I knew it, I knew it. ☺

11 Likes, 5 Comments

------Trust your gut when it comes to a Lab this age ☺ Dexter ate my car bumper when I knew I should not let him sleep in the garage one afternoon......

------lol there's long and more mischief days/weeks/or months to come for us having a headache with our puppies sometimes!

------*Men don't listen....they never worry about nothing...at least my male species doesn't, lol*

------*Get a bigger crate......*

------*Husbands really should listen more often.*

August 9

Another weird sleeping position with eyes open...

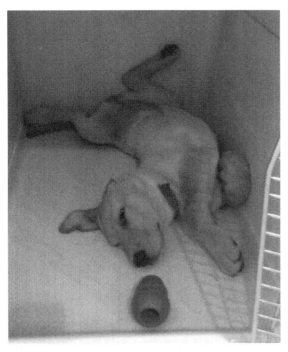

6 Likes, 15 comments

------*Life is ruff in the Cyrus house isn't it!!!*

------*keeping her eye on that Kong treat!*

------She is rotten! Don't you wish you could twist like that?

------Hahahahaha! She is made of rubber!

------My 13-year-old English springer spaniel sleeps like that all the time.

------she is just a real puppy......

August 11

For the next two weeks you won't see all the cutesy stuff on Della because we'll be out of town and the in-laws will stay here to dogsit. So the next time you see a picture or video, Della will be much bigger and hopefully more trainable.

0 Likes, 7 Comments

------aaaaaawwwwwwwwwwwwwwww say it isn't so.

------You come home to a spoiled dog!

------I will miss seeing Della's antics for two weeks!!!

------I can't imagine being apart from lil Bella for that long!

------bad mommy! Leaving your baby behind.

August 12

I have to remind myself that I am too old to have separation anxiety from my puppy, thanks to my boss's suggestion. Like everyone else, she assured that Della will be fine under my in-laws' care for two weeks. Now...Maine, here I come!

3 Likes, 5 Comments

------how about the in-laws?

------(Bainy replies) Jeanette has hit it off with Della and insisted that she had raised two boys so she knows what she is doing!

------and when you get back lil miss Della will be HUGE!!! Have fun Bainy! ☺

------As a dog mother, I can tell you you're never going to go away and not think (and worry) about your furry child, but the reunion is as good as it gets.

------Your parents and a puppy, I'd fear for them, not the puppy! lol

August 16

Spoke to in-laws back at home and they're thoroughly enjoying their granddogs Della and Mabel. They can handle 11 more days of dogsitting since Della no longer whines in the middle of night to pee. Bladder has gotten bigger. So has she...

3 Likes, 4 Comments

------She's going to keep getting bigger until she's about 100 pounds. Big puppy paws!

------Bainy, I am thoroughly enjoying the escapades of your pup! Hope you're enjoying your vacation...especially now that you know you will be sleeping through the night when you get home!

------me too it brings back memories of Sunshine was a little ball of fur

------When Bailiff came home his paws were so big for him he could barely walk!

August 21

Steve's 80-something mother assured that she is having a blast babysitting Della and that she herself hasn't aged a bit. I guess a puppy is the best anti-aging treatment for anyone...

13 Likes, 4 Comments

------*She sounds wonderful! Perhaps a Maine lobster dinner care package for granddog sitting!?!*

------*So true!*

------*Mom's started to hint that she'd like another dog since having to put Sadie down...However, she's given me the same criteria: Spayed female, small, housebroken and a little older so as not to deal with training a puppy...Sadie fell into our lap like a miracle! Here's to hoping miracles happen twice!* ☺

------*So good to know she can do it and you can vacation!*

August 27

Della's first hurricane. Calm as can be.

7 Likes, 9 Comments

------*She is really growing*

------*Such a precious dog...Bainy, those paws are HUGE!*

------*she is so precious!! thinking about ya'll in the storm!*

------*What a beautiful, pensive face.*

------*Cute! And bigger now. How are u all doing with the hurricane in Norfolk?*

------*That dog is beautiful! Hope u all are handling the storm alright!*

------*looks like Della has grown a bit in a short time.*

August 27

Family Album

Della Whitten – Steve's granny

Della Cyrus – Great Granddog

2 Likes, 4 Comments

------*Wonderful...*

------*Too cool!*

------*Aw, I think there's a little resemblance there; both beautiful ladies!*

-----*I LOVE that portrait of Mrs. Whitten. Beautiful.*

August 27

A puppy and Facebook have kept me out of boredom during this long waiting day... (Waiting for Hurricane Irene to pass)

10 Likes, 1 Comment

------*We have a terrified Jack Russell and a bored beagle-mix puppy. I just came in from the barn...big surprise, the chicken didn't lay today!*

September 1

A three-month-old Lab can be extremely stubborn when walking on a leash, stopping every two feet to sniff, sniff, sniff, and even lie down in rebellion. Should I dangle a carrot in front of her nose?

0 Likes, 9 Comments

------*That wouldn't work, now a nice steak maybe...*

------*We bought the gentle leader. They used it with Hazel at camp.*

------*(Bainy replies) Not a bad idea, Elizabeth. Will have to buy one this weekend. Thanks!*

------*Have you ever watched The Dog Whisperer?*

------*He's just checking his pee-mail!*

------*Train her off the leash! It's much easier!*

------*Lol, yes, gentle leader helps, Elizabeth.*

------*Hi again, Bainy, I realize it isn't practical to train her off leash but may I suggest that you teach her that walks are for exercise by keeping her to heel until the last five minutes of the walk when she is then free to sniff and mark? She is so young to start but short little walks around the block at heel and then the freedom to sniff might ba a good start.*

------*get puppies for dummies*

September 2

What, Della?

4 Likes, 10 Comments

------*I believe the universal translation of that is: Please Mommy, LET ME OUT!*

------*"Lemme out, I want to play!"*

------*Mommy, mommy, I am ready to go now. Thanks for my break but I am ready for the rest of the day. Thanks, mommy.*

------*OMG! How can you resist that face!!!*

------*Adorable, but she'll soon be able to either climb over or knock it down.*

------*Boy, are you lucky Della's not jumping over that gate. Calvin is a Lhasa Aspo/Terrier mixed and if I leave him home, I have to stack 2 baby gates up at the kitchen doorway and one in the kitchen/dining room pass through the window. Yep! It takes 3 baby gates to keep him in the kitchen. He's an escape artist!*

September 3

A dog is supposed to chase the ball, at least stay dry. Della just got into the fishpond and chased goldfishes...

7 Likes, 5 Comments

------Love it! GO Della and continue keeping your parents on their toes; it's good for them!

------(Bainy replies) She even buried her face in the muddy shallow water by the waterfall and her face was black!

------Things that dogs do!

------Rotflmaoff!

------my lab puppy bailiff used to retrieve lunch bags from sacred heart school and run home with the patrol boy chasing behind! I love labs. Della is adorable

September 4

Della seems to have a strong appetite for Steve's homegrown eggplants. She steals them before we can ever make eggplant parmigiana. Aren't dogs supposed to eat their dog food???

0 Likes, 3 Comments

------have you ever tasted their dog food? Even eggplant would taste good compared to that!

------My dog is a veggie-hound too. LOL Maybe it's good I didn't grow a garden this year.

------Have you ever tasted that stuff nasty!!! Sunshine loves fruit and picks strawberries right off the vine.

September 5

Hummingbirds are amazing: they attack each other over the feeder. I swear I saw three of them swoop down toward unsuspecting Della and then rocket back up to keep chasing each other. That scared poor Della – she must've thought those hummies were giant bumblebees. (Yes, she was stung once and knows for sure what a bee is!)

2 Likes, 2 Comments

------I love hummingbirds too – and have seen them be aggressive towards each other. They are so fast!

September 5

Puppy teeth, can you hurry up and get less sharper?

0 Likes, 5 Comments

------Cow hooves have worked great to wear the sharpness down on our horse..., I mean Goldendoodle (4 mo. Old and 40 lbs)

------lol yah I know! I kept buying her (my puppy) teething toys, but still she is a very mouthy one that drove us crazy...the book said that retriever dogs are the most mouthy ones.

------(Bainy replies) Maybe I ought to get Della a fake duck?

------King Kong!

------soft toys make for a soft bite in retrievers, the desirable result.

September 8

What to do with a bored puppy on a rainy day? Throw a small cardboard box on the kitchen floor. No wonder Della is attacking it now while I am at peace on this computer.

2 Likes, 2 Comments

------(Bainy adds) She did better than a paper shredder.

------lol even my retriever pup doesn't like getting wet and I kept telling her "huh yer supposed to love water, but still you're icky when it comes to the rain!" Yet, she looked at me like "no way I aint going out in the rain!"

September 10

Della is having a great time in the ocean but spends a lot of time chasing seagulls and watching the birds above her. She's probably destined to be a L.L. Bean hunting dog but Steve and I are not into that sport. Della can still retrieve the ball, not a duck.

3 Likes, 3 Comments

------She'll always be interested in birds; it's in her nature. But she won't be missing anything not to be part of a hunt. Let her fetch her ball, and toys; and please, please, please keep posting pictures of that beautiful girl ☺

------come to Raleigh, we can chase tennis balls in the Falls Lake

------Eventually she will figure out that she is not going to catch a bird and then she'll pay more attention to tennis balls and sticks. In the meantime take her somewhere that there is a hill and let her chase the birds and

watch her look of confusion as they fly away and she runs down the hill all the while getting further away from them.

September 13

What?

14 Likes, 10 Comments

------*Puppy legs!*

------*That's what my ex and I used to call "the sloppy sit"*

September 14

My plan for this finally cool weather: Prune all the shrubs, secure the fishpond rocks, remove all the finished veggie plants, yank out the fish net from tomato plants, pull out wilting summer annuals, and on and on...More important, make the yard more puppyproof.

3 Likes, 5 Comments

------*Good luck on your last wish!*

------*...or, you could just let your puppy loose in the yard and let him take care of all that for you...then puppyproof!*

------*Sounds like a plan! What time will you be here to start?*

September 17

Rain, rain, rain...how can I get rid of the wet dog smell? I mean, not only Della and Mabel but also me!

0 Likes, 4 Comments

------*Swim in a warm swimming pool.*

------*You can't, so just go with it, LOL! You love dogs, you love water, use those positive associations to handle the smell. The smell of the ocean is not exactly pretty but we beach lovers all love it because of what it means to us. Like pet hair on your clothes, it can make you crazy or you can own it; I call it my favorite accessory. Aren't I helpful?!*

------*LOL...It's a battle you can't win! Mine have created their own bare dirt digging and playing area and come back in the house and shake it off....Today that's area is a mud bath!*

------*Rub that cute dog down with Bounce dryer sheets!*

September 19

Imagine spending an almost full day with over 20 partying dogs at the doggie daycare - in an open playroom and without a single second of napping. Ask Della but you have to wait until tomorrow morning when she is AWAKE!

6 Likes, 3 Comments

------(From Jana the owner of Happy Tails) Laughing... wait until you see the pictures! Make sure to see all of them.

------(Bainy replies) Amazing! Thanks! Glad Della swam today.

------We had a doggie daycare near my old office and when I needed a good heart warming laugh and fun during the day I'd go over and watch all the wonderful sweet adorable kind dogs at play. It was the best part of a day.

September 19

Good Lord, Della is dressed up as a submarine at Happy Tails. Thanks, Jana, for your awesome daily pics!

19 Likes, 15 Comments

------*oh no.....I see doggie Halloween looming!*

------*Della looks thrilled!*

------*how could she be so big so soon?!*

------*(Bainy replies) Corn flakes.*

------*now I have to bring Reggie there to play.*

------*I'm thinking that Susie (who is 14 years old in people years) would NOT have a good time with all of those youngsters!!!!!!LOL*

------*Too cute!!! I love this! I'm so ready to get another puppy! It's been since May...*

------That is a riot, a retriever wearing a life jacket :)

------So cute!!! She is growing like a weed!!!

September 22

Golly, with Steve gone for a week hiking in CA, I feel like I'm in the sandwich generation - taking care of a four-month old puppy and a 15-year-old mutt. Now Steve is finally, finally coming home in a few hours and I'll finally, finally be relieved of some duties at 5:30 in the morning and overnight...

4 Likes, 1 Comment

------wee now you can have your extra beauty sleep in every other day ;) I've been there, too! Lol

September 24

Trying to put eye drops on a suspicious four-month-old puppy is like the water gun game where you try to shoot into a clown's mouth to inflate a balloon. Not easy.

5 Likes, 0 Comments

September 27

Della is all kissy kissy at Happy Tails

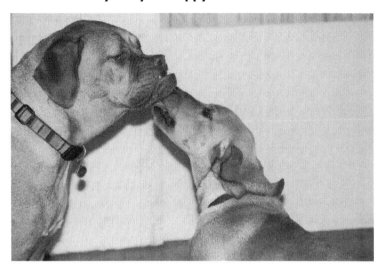

17 Likes, 4 Comments

------*this is just the sweetest picture EVER!* ☺

------*Great seeing you today!* ☺

------*What a great picture!*

------*how adorable!*

September 28

Exhausted from Doggie Daycare

20 Likes, 11 Comments

------*I love this dog....*

------*Aww... do you take her to Day Care every day while you work? except weekends off that your dog would love it!! :-)*

------*(Bainy replies) Not every day. Most of the time 3X during the week, sometimes 4th in the last minute. And it's not all day, just 3-5 hours at a time. Della loves it!*

------*A tired puppy is a well behaved puppy.*

------*I believe she's ready for a bigger crate.*

------This made me laugh this morning!

------That's great. Like a rottie, a tired lab is a happy lab. lol

September 30

There has never been a day when I don't have to put my entire hand in Della's mouth to find a foreign object in there. Two days ago it was a plant label; yesterday it was my computer mouse; today it was a Steve's small sprinkler head; tomorrow will be...God knows what else...

3 Likes, 9 Comments

------a whole loaf of bread, a wooden tiki torch or maybe a breast of chicken just about ready to go on the grill...

------Hutch ate my glasses :(I know the feeling...

------(From Jana the owner of Happy Tails) It's so much more interesting on my end... the things we find in poo. My all time favorite was a Victoria Secret Thong!

------Our first dog would eat anything.....his particular favorites were undies fresh out of the laundry. Which he would then deposit, in their entirety, on neighbors' lawns in the Fan. Soooooo embarassing!

------(Bainy comments) I've heard a story in which the wife, a traveling businesswoman, found out that her husband had been entertaining an escort in their own house while she was away. How? She found a lace underwear in their dog's poop and knew it was not hers!

------Hide the remote controls they love to eat them.

------Mango had a sticky pad in her mouth a minute ago. . .

------lol oh yes I've been there to nowdays, aren't they very MOUTHY!? geez I never vacuumed this much like about everyday since we got the puppy, and making sure that nothing's foreign on the floors, etc, but when it comes to outside, god help us! lol (Della and my Bella are only few weeks apart :) Heard that it won't stop till about a year old, oh man I can't wait when they reach this age!

------In the store the other night, Brogan ate allllll the garden gloves, my garden shoes, a rubber mallet and two hammers....guess the chewing brings comfort!!!

October 2

Good Morning....we're now prepping Della and Mabel for the animal blessing at our church. As she's done it for the past 13 years, Mabel knows how to sit in the pew behavorially and let the minister rub a cross on her forehead. Della? Well, I don't know. It'd be very interesting...

9 Likes, 4 Comments

------Good Shepherd? (Yes)

------Let me know how it goes.

------Good Luck

------Hope she didn't eat the cross!

October 2

Della made it through her first Animal Blessing at the Church of Good Shepherd OK. It took several minutes for her to calm and sit properly in the pew - although she tried to eat a hymn sheet. I had to throw it over to the next pew. At least Della has been blessed as a puppy.

11 Likes, 3 Comments

------*I think YOU are the one who is blessed with such a precious dog! I love reading about her adventures! Glad to see that she is properly blessed for future adventures!*

------*She was precious!*

------*still "mouthy" pup :) god bless her..wished we have a place for our dogs to go to for blessings, I'm gonna ask my minister about it next week!*

October 2

More on Della: She'd developed a phobia of lawn mowers, often hiding in a bush as far as she could go. Every time she saw a mower in the neighborhood, she'd cower behind my legs or try to run away. So I decided to try dog therapy over the weekend. That's what you call exposure treatment. While Steve was mowing only several feet away, I held on to Della and tried to comfort her. The longer she was exposed to our mower, the less frantic she became. Finally she had the guts to approach the thrown ball on the lawn while Steve continued mowing a few feet away!

8 Likes, 8 Comments

------*Aw we already exposed Bella to lawn mower and vacuum, she tried to chase them!*

------Good work Bainy!

------That makes a better dog. Your patience worked !!!!!!!

------I have also seen where tying a string around the dog's tail and when the dog starts to tuck her tail you pull the tail up signals the dog to not be scared and to not go into a frightened posture...sort of an interesting concept. When my child was scared of new people I did the same thing ... put my fingers under her chin...made her look up and say, "Hello." And now she is a regular politician!

------If it works , go for it. LOL at the Miss Regular Politician !!!!!!

------you are such a good mom!

------Just don't get her so comfortable that she gets in front of the mower, but that's not likely to happen. I do Prolonged Exposure Therapy with my PTSD patients, kind of like what you did.

October 5

Guess what was on my doorstep this morning??? The 12th Yellow Pages of the year!!! Oh, what a waste of trees...Since I already have a few phone books that we've never used, I threw this new one to Della on the kitchen floor. She's no longer bored and now attacking that phone book. She's doing trees a favor.

4 Likes, 0 Comments

October 6

(Bainy added a new photo)

22 Likes, 5 Comments

------*OMG*

------*How could you possibly resist that face?!*

------*So sweet! Waiting for her glass of wine!!! lol*

------*Bainy, you must realize how truly special this sweet dog is....we love her simply through her pictures. Hope to meet her one day.*

------*Sweet, but Della may be mad.... figure out... you can see what it is behind Della!*

October 6

Took Della to the Oceanfront in this gorgeous weather. She has yet to take interest in the water since she still has a lot of exploration to do on the beach. She even considered eating an upside-down dead horseshoe crab but thought better of it. Della went on to dig a deep hole in the sand and buried her face in it and then went around to the other side and dug another hole, refilling the one she had just dug. Back and forth. So the beach is still safe for anyone to walk on.

4 Likes, 3 Comments

------*i love della*

------*What a delightful and thrilling experience! I have introduced Mango to the lake in Canada, but not the ocean or bay yet.*

------*Daisy and Riddick like to eat the jellyfish that wash up on the floor and then barf them up in the back of my car on the way home. Yummy.*

October 8

Oh geez, my poor little sweet Della looks like a gang dog - with her new prong collar...

0 Likes, 13 Comments

------*You will love that thing!*

------*what are the advantages of a prong collar?*

------*Dislike! I am dead set against the use of prong collars. More and more trainers feel the same these days.*

------*I had to get one for my 6-mo.old golden a couple of months ago. I originally was not for it but after testing it on my own arm, I realized it doesn't hurt the dog - it's more pressure than anything. It's to replicate a mother correcting her pup. After trying other types of collars, it has been the ONLY method that has worked for our trainer and us in training him how to walk, not jump on people, etc. Good luck!*

------I have seen lots of energetic large dogs when it made the difference between control or not. They seldom had to be used for control once the dog realized who the "Alpha" was, and once the dog completed a successful six week training class.

------Bainy, dog trainers run the gamut from certified and current to having little to no training at all. I think it's always a good idea to educate yourself through reading the most up-to-date information out there. Use a trainer for guidance but also go with your gut and what you've learned on your own. Our understanding of dogs and how they best learn has, thankfully, come a long way over the years, and there has been a good deal of recent progress. The most current belief is we do not need to be the "Alpha" (I just read a long article on that) or use pain, discomfort, force or any other harsh method to teach our dogs. These methods may get a faster response but may also create fear and distrust and can backfire in the long run. Dogs want to please their people and the most effective approach for positive, long term results is repetition and reward. In training them this way, you build trust and a wonderful friendship.

------One more thing. I really emphasize to go with your gut and trust your instincts, because I didn't always do that and regret it to this day. When I first started training dogs back in the 80s I blindly followed the trainers. I attended one class with a trainer who was well-respected at the time. He used my dog as an example of teaching a down-stay which my little guy had resisted. He put his foot on the leash close to the collar and held it there while my dog flipped around and yelped and finally submitted. I did not like it, felt sick to my stomach, made a weak objection but let it happen. From then on my dog always went into a down-stay in a split second and with fear in his eyes leaving me feeling guilty for not standing up for my

dog and what I knew in my heart was wrong. I currently have a dog whose previous owner used a prong collar for training. This dog (who has now been with me for 5 yrs) may be worse than usual, but still, every time I touch his soft collar in the gentlest way he cries out as if I've done something awful. It makes me sad.

------it works quickly

October 9

Della has socialized with an Irish Wolfhound, a huge teeth-baring boxer, two rockhard bull terriers, a humongous Labradoodle, a neighborhood Golden retriever, and ten daycare Labs four times her size. Sounds like a brave puppy. But a horse? She saw one for the first time today at a relative's farm and didn't know what the hell a horse was. Scared? Yes.

4 Likes, 3 Comments

------Convince her it's just a really big dog. LOL

------(From Nora the breeder) She was born on a horse farm, but never got too close to them. I was afraid she might get stepped on when she was younger, not knowing that she should get away.

------(Bainy replies) Now she knows to get away!

October 11

Went to the drive-thru at the bank with Della yelping and barking in the back. She was anxious to get moving to Happy Tails for daycare. After the transaction was done, I opened the box and there was a deposit slip, some cash - and a dog biscuit. I was touched because I thought banks gave only lollipops for kids!

18 Likes, 16 Comments

------*I love it.. So sweet from the sweet teller!! :-))*

------*I used to have the tellers do that at Suntrust. We even gave one to a guy at the ATM...talk about being shocked when a hand came out of the slot with a dog biscuit...priceless!!!*

------*Out here, dogs are welcome most everywhere - inside the banks, stores, shops, etc. Most everyone offers dog treats, and one of my dogs has (with the tellers'/shop keepers' encouragement) developed the habit of putting his feet up on the counter as soon as we walk in looking for his treat.*

------*Old Point gives dog biscuits out also! The dogs start to expect it like the kids expect lollipops!*

------*The UPS guy leaves treats for our dogs when he drops off a package.*

------*the tails are always a waggin`on my doggies when they hear the mail man.....*

------*They give dog biscuits at the Chesapeake Bay Tunnel too!*

------*walgreens gives out doggie treats at the pharmacy drive-through*

------*Your bank has a drive thru??*

------*(Bainy replies) Yes, Jen. I bet they don't in Australia, do they?*

------*(Jen replies) Gotta say, it seems to me that drive thru's are an American concept. The only drive thru's we have here are maccas (mcdonalds) and kfc and they're not Australian!*

October 11

We were having a quiet dinner in the dining room last night but then Steve heard Della whining and moaning as if she was in pain. So we ran over to see what was going on. Della was fine. She was flat on her side, legs twitching - sound asleep and dreaming about some activity at the daycare.

5 Likes, 2 Comments

------*Bainy, that's common on dogs sleeping and sounding like they are crying inside while sleeping. my dog, Princess does that quite often. Its so sweet to hear that they are really just dreaming.*

------*I always say they are chasing rabbits*

October 12

Waiting for daycare...

20 Likes, 18 Comments

------*A tired puppy is a well behaved puppy*

------*What a doll.*

------*I once had a foster dog (black lab) who I took to doggy daycare, because he could jump my fence and was not getting enough exercise on the leash. After 2 weeks at daycare, he was wilder than ever, so I asked the daycare providers why they thought that was. They told me that he jumped their fences, too, so had to spend his days in the TV room watching 101 Dalmations.*

------*I love your posts and pictures of Della, makes me smile all the time.*

------*c o m m e r c i a l*

------*Della makes me SMILE!*

------*Will she ever grow into those feet and legs?*

------*I bet she thinks she is going to Happy Tails*

October 13

Had a scare with Della this morning. She broke a small glass dish despite its out of reach on the counter and apparently swallowed a small shard before Steve rushed there. At the daycare they found a little blood in her stool but said she appeared to be OK, still playing hard and eating her whole lunch. Thanks to Jana and Lisa for their observance and suggestion for a cottonball treatment. You just dip a couple of these fluffy balls in peanut butter and then they will wrap around a sharp object during bowel movement, making the passage safer. Now I've got to make the kitchen free of glass and start using paper plates!

0 Likes, 12 Comments

------*I understand! Had a Perfect Dog, then Got Brownie that she was like a Problem Child, but getting better as gets older! Lots of work and freaked me out! The other Dog used to chew power cords! That one scared me!!!! Big Spanks, had to! ; (*

------*Had a Chesapeake Bay Retriever that ate a beer can once. Found shards of can in her poop but she seemed fine after the "pass through".*

------*(Bainy replies) Good Grief...Dogs eat weird stuff, don't they?*

------*Daisy ate a tube of red paint that I had out on my palette after she had a small operation at the vet. .When I came in and she had blood all over her face and her victorian collar, I thought she had ripped open her stitches. scared me to death. It wasn't toxic (I called poison control) but it looked like Play-doh through an extruder in the backyard the second time around....*

------(From same person with the beer can dog) She used to eat her own poop too until the vet told me to put meat tenderizer on her food. For some reason that solved the problem and it improved her breath dramatically.

------That is for Sure!!!!!!

------Never heard the cotton ball trick...

------Baby, child and now dog proof the home. Glad she is okay.

------Hope she is okay. Cotton ball idea is very smart.

------oh no...that cute thing getting into something again??? Hope she didn't eat too many peanuts.

------Oh that cotton ball idea to wrap around a sharp object is good try, hope she's ok, isn't she? Yea tell me about how careful we should be with our puppies like getting paper plates instead, my lil Bella grabbed a thumbtack the other day, and luckily my husband took it out of her mouth quickly which was almost down in her throat! As he swiped this sign on the door with thumbtacks and one of two was dropped on the floor that Bella ran and grabbed it so fast!

------Freda, a beer can? Oh my good gracious! Are you sure that it isn't a goat, but a dog? :) You know that dogs loved beeeer!

October 13

Still trying to get over the glass-eating drama. Della seems to be OK, still burying her head in the dog food bag. Now, guys, can you tell me why dogs have such a strange appetite for anything unfortified from bank card to underwear? Homework is alright for me because I'm done with school. But still...why?

1 Like, 7 Comments

------*Dogs like chewing on things. Get some nybones (not rawhides) for her to chew on. They last a while and can take on chewing.*

------*Who knows. Perhaps not a discriminating palate! My puppy is the same way. Teach her the "leave it" command.*

------*When our sweet yellow Lab Dorothy was little -- she ate two pairs of glasses (prescription), the remote control for the TV, all of the shoes out of our cousin's suitcase, opened (but did not eat) over 35 Christmas presents, and pulled toilet paper off the roll and scattered it throughout the house. Did I mention gnawing on the legs of the dining room table?*

------*My mom woke up one afternoon from a nap to find her pup chewing on her dentures....ewwwwww!*

------*You did read "Marley and Me", didn't you?*

------*I had both a cat and a dog eaten my earmolds (and once my hearing aid) in the past. I now lock them every night in a drawer.*

October 15

Della did fine in her second obedience class early this morning as long as she could get a treat after each command. But there is one thing she really needs to learn: GENTLY pick up a treat, not bite my hand off.

2 Likes, 1 Comment

------*close your hand around the treat w/ the top of your hand up~only turn your hand over and open up when she is calmer...she will learn some patience ~ it will take time but be consistent = don't reward her enthusiasm, only release the treat when she is quiet!*

October 15

Steve just told me his good friend's English Lab ate a hearing aid. I wonder if that dog can now hear better? Della better not eat mine! I cannot afford to lose any more hearing! (FYI, I was born hard-of-hearing and have been wearing hearing aids all my life.)

6 Likes, 8 Comments

------*Gah! What an expensive meal!*

------*(Bainy replies) No kidding! Costs more than a 52" flatscreen TV!*

------*Plus dogs often like the earmold(s)!*

------*Oh yes Bainy, my dog Princess when she was a puppy, she practically chewed up my hearing aid. the mold was gone.*

------*I seem to remember that one of our dogs ate Meredith's hearing aid.*

------*(From Bainy's audiologist Angela) It's one of the most frequent causes of lost hearing aids!!*

------*I believe that my dog ate one of my molds before I switched over to hard clear molds. Now that i have CIs my cat leaves them alone but they have been known to be chewed on also by animals.*

------*My dog once chewed the dome off my open fit hearing aid but luckily i just had to replace the tubing and not the whole hearing aid itself. that would have been about another $1250.*

October 17

During my annual physical exam this morning my doc came back in after reading my EKG results and said, "After walking your puppy four times a day, your heart is in perfect shape." Well, I'm really thrilled...thanks, Della.

9 Likes, 6 Comments

------*Am happy 4 u. thanks to Della 4 such a perfect job.*

------*people with dogs live longer. for real! an added bonus above and beyond all the other ones!*

------*Is Della for rent? I could use some help.*

October 18

Happy Tails Doggie Daycare with constant activity can really develop nice biceps...

14 Likes, 2 Comments

------*Very buff!*

------*Della is adorable!*

October 20

It's finally 54 degrees and Della is wagging her tail during the whole walk. Originated in Newfoundland, Labradors are supposed to be out in the cold!

2 Likes, 1 Comment

------(From a friend with a toy poodle) Even Mango is energized!

October 20

Took Della to work with me, checking on a few clients in Suffolk. Though she stayed in the back of the car with a squeaky toy, Della was a well-behaved sidekick. Then we were back in Norfolk for a windy walk at Town Point Park. The rough water scared Della briefly but she went on sniffing what was left over on the grass from last weekend's Wine Festival. Then she approached a lifesize bronze statue of a young military family embracing in a homecoming salute and wondered why those people didn't move. That dog has got a lot to learn.

4 Likes, 1 Comment

------I love reading about her adventures! We can learn from her...

October 21

Something scares me about Della. I noticed that the bone on top of her head had tripled in size overnight. Steve wonders if it's a normal growth pattern but I wonder if she hit her head in her grate while dreaming, though Della doesn't flinch when I touch it. Della looks like a Saturday Night Live Conehead. Is that normal???

0 Likes, 8 Comments

------*No. Not normal. Vet time.*

------*I'd call a vet.*

------*Nope, could be a cyst.*

------*(Bainy replies) We're now at the vet. Will let you know*

------*Just checked our Layla. She has a big boney head AND she is a big bonehead too. But check it out to ease your mind.*

------*Hope she's OK.*

------*Any word yet?*

------*Keep us posted*

October 20 (Two hours later)

Back from the vet. Della is OK but did hit her head hard, possibly under the kitchen table early this morning. The vet drew some fluid from the bump, tested it, and concluded that it is not hematoma or infected. What Della has is seroma - it's a collection of fluid under the skin. It'll eventually go away without treatment in about ten days or so but no wrestling with other dogs in the meantime. So she'll look like a conehead for a while...Thanks to some of you for your helpful suggestions in the earlier post. The vet said she was glad I posted Della's accident on Facebook so I would know. What a morning...

11 Likes, 9 Comments

------*Great news and I know that you are relieved that she is fine!*

------*I'm glad she's going to be OK. You made a good call - always better to be on the safe side with our 4-legged friends.*

------Oh I'm glad you took her to the vet just to be assured than sorry. Poor dizzy Della :/

------Good News! Watch out for that cone- it will leave a nasty bruise if she gets you with it.

------YEA!!!!!!!! good news. No playing with other dogs for a few days. Glad the doctor liked you sharing on facebook!!!!!!!!!!

------ should we take bets? Will this be the last playground/rough house injury energetic Della incurs?

------my parents' dog has had those in her ear-retriever with floppy ears that get hurt while playing-I'm so glad that everything is all right...

October 23

Why did I remove most of the magnets/pics and move the rest to the top? Because Della ate my nephew's picture.

5 Likes, 6 Comments

------*still not high enough up to keep a lab from getting what she wants.*

------*Bainy, I found a large piece of metal air conditioner grate in the garage by Brogan today......argh.....*

------*just a little heads up---that probably won't be the last non food item she eats. Sunshine and Ginger ate all the pillows and blankets in the house, chewed a Turkish rug, countless shoes.... and broke the springs in 2 sofas playing queen of the mountain--for more insight watch 'Marley and Me'*

------*My lab learned to open the frig and helped herself to the contents whenever the opportunity presented itself.*

------*At least she didn't eat your nephew.*

------*remember that Della will never get more mature than about 2-4 years old.... it will never change...*

October 24

Gorgeous outside. I'm writing casenotes and preparing for the book tour here on the brick patio under the awning while Della is frolicking in the grass and chasing squirrels. The problem is, whenever I have to go to the bathroom or want a snack, I have to take everything back inside for a few minutes. I don't trust Della with my laptop!

6 Likes, 2 Comments

------*Good Call!*

------*You're so funny! I've got to meet this dog!*

October 25

Yes, the Nike warm-up pants are quite stylish and very comfortable but they are certainly a magnet for yellow dog hair.

0 Likes, 4 Comments

------*That's a fashion statement for dog lovers.*

------*(Bainy comments) I can't even wipe it off...*

------*Before you know it, you'll have sticky lint rollers in every room! Buy in bulk at Costco...*

------*Denim, graphic t shirts and denim....*

October 27

Della turns five months old today. See if you can do the calculation in dog/human years and decide if she is over the terrible twos...I don't think so. I'll give her one more month...

1 Like, 8 Comments

------*one more month? ahh I don't think so, I'd give her another 6 months! Lol*

------*LOL. I'd bet 12 more months minimally!*

------*After seeing the doggy gates? I think it'll be another year before she's over the terrible twos.*

------*I think three years before you can be sure :)*

------*(Bainy comments) Aw, c'mon, guys...I think you're all contracting dog years too severely.*

------*Tell my three-legged Chippendale dining room chair that... :-)*

------*nah she's a retriever, they take waaaaay longer to mature*

------*Just be glad she's not a "real" person...21 years and we're still not sure!!*

October 30

Here I was, drinking coffee, reading a big fat Sunday paper, and watching 'Good Morning, America'...Oh, so relaxing...Then I felt huge thumps. The horse had been released by mischievous Steve. Galloping up the stairs and rattling the whole house. Here came Della flying onto my bed but luckily after I had the speed-of-light sense to put my coffee on the table. She's gotten so big that my bed felt like a trampoline. Now I've got to shake off all the dog hair. Thanks, Steve...

11 Likes, 12 Comments

------*I have big dogs, too, Bainy! Know that scenario well!*

------*That is a good welcome home greeting!*

------*Love this........I can close my eyes and imagine the scene.....*

------*(Bainy comments) Imagine this scenario in slow motion with Della in midair toward my bed and my coffee in midair toward the table...*

------*never a dull moment with a dog in the house!*

------*I let Reggie out early this frosty am and of course he went swimming?? He has no limits!*

------*"mischievous Steve" two most important words in the post! He has not changed! haha. Have a fun rest of the weekend with your TWO puppies!*

October 30

Dogs have an advantage of not being able to talk or even lie. Before Steve got home, I fed both Della and Mabel big bowls of dinner. Then I went upstairs to take a shower. Steve came home and fed Della and Mabel two more big bowls of dinner, not knowing that I'd already fed them. Human error, not pet...We're going to pay the price with extra poop bags.

9 Likes, 6 Comments

------*this has happened more than once with Holly and Layla. You would think they would say to us, "but Mom already fed us"- ha ha.*

------*Lucky dogs!!*

------*That happened to me, too so from now on it'll be just me feeding them! now my hubby gets jealous cause he wanted to be the one being well loved and favored by the dogs!*

------*Double duty. (doody)*

------*Meagan tries to "snooker" us all the time....she can act sooooo hungry :)*

------*don't be so sure. Daisy and Riddick and Captain are always pretending they haven't been fed in DAYS when they were fed 5 minutes ago. they get double fed all the time!*

October 31

Della's Tri-Kiss at Happy Tails

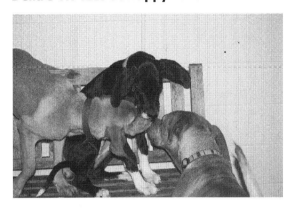

6 Likes, 3 Comments

------that's too racy for FB

------It's a menagerie-a-trois!

November 1

It's been four weeks since I started using a prong collar on Della only for walks and it has worked remarkably well as long as I don't tug her too hard. She has become more mannerly, no longer chasing other dogs or sniffing poops left on grass or jumping on little old ladies. Don't be feared by that mean-looking collar. It's actually harmless if placed above a regular collar as recommended and does not choke at all. Try pressing a hard plastic hairbrush face-down on your arm. That's what it feels like on a dog's neck. Only pressure, not punctures. And you can still breathe through it. No wonder Della walks like a lady...

5 Likes, 3 Comments

------It is a great tool, Bainy...We have used them with all our puppies....and we use it still when we walk Casey, our golden :-)

------they work good on kids too...

November 2

Hope you don't mind me posting something about Della nearly everyday but puppyhood sure is interesting. She doesn't seem to have enough to eat. We have increased the amount of expensive 100% fortified puppy food from a "heaping" cup to almost two. I mean, THREE times a day. But still after each meal Della either tries to eat her bowl or break into the pantry to bury her head in the puppy food bag. She eats like an elephant and I'm afraid she's going to get that big!

2 Likes, 11 Comments

------WORMS

------(Bainy replies) I don't think so because Della has had all the shots and regularly takes heartworm pills. She's just an active puppy and I believe she'll be a tall Lab since she has nice long legs.

------(From Jana of Happy Tails Daycare) That is totally normal. Don't worry Bainy.

------(Bainy comments) So, Jana, you've seen how FAST Della eats at your daycare. I'm sure it's entertaining for you guys!

------(Jana replies) Not the fastest eater we have ever seen.... but pretty darn quick!

------She's a growing girl so feed her now so she won't be like that when she's older. My Golden that I free fed can take it or leave it but my rescue girl wants to eat everything in sight all the time and she's 8 now.

------Branigan at sixteen weeks is up to six cups a day plus treats!

------I recommend PETWAY. All natural food, delivered to your door. No fillers - no gas! Very nice people, too!

------dogs will eat whatever you put in front of them...with gusto! good luck!

------my only recommendation is keep her underweight until she's at least 12 mos old so her hips can fully develop without excess weight. coming from a guy who had a 110 lb english lab :)

November 2

Oh no, already a lapdog...

25 Likes, 12 Comments

------soon she'll be your 85 lb. lap dog...lol!

------always a lap dog :)

------mine is already a lap dog, too! Can Della jump over the fence yet? My Bella hasn't figured it out yet! Don't want nor ready for her doing that yet!

------she's huge!!!! and cute!

------i thought you weren't letting Della out of the kitchen for another year.

------Spoiled....not Della but the green jacket fella ;)

------That's going to be tough on the legs when she is huge!

November 3

November is a good time to find a parking space right by the access to the beach, take the dog out, and play with the dog on a vast empty beach. No parking tickets, no crowds, or no dog rules...I let Della do whatever she darn well pleased. She dug deep holes, ran in all directions, tested the rough shore, and frolicked in the white foams. Yes, she went number two, a big one, but the bag took care of it. We didn't break any rules and she had a blast!

13 Likes, 1 Comment

------My favorite time of year!

November 4

Quite a day...I was driving Della home from daycare when a Lee's Friends patient phoned a half hour early to say she was done with her chemotherapy. Not wanting to make this sweet little old lady wait longer, I decided to drive straight ahead to the clinic and pick her up. And explained why I had a puppy sleeping in the back. Just then Della passed gas, stinking up the whole car. As a dedicated volunteer, I profusely apologized to the lady but she waved it off and said, "I am a 100% dog person" and showed me pictures of her beloved Scottish terriers. She didn't even pinch her nose so that was good...

25 Likes, 0 Comments

November 6

Oh geez...Della has started doing something most Labradors and other breeds do: Eat poop. Now that she's spent more time in our fenced yard, she eats the other dog Mabel's poop. I've been told by a few friends to sprinkle meat tenderizer on it since it repels dogs for good so I'm going to try this method. Not only that but also pick up all the poop we can find in our yard, prevent Della from sniffing poop during neighborhood walks, and consult with the vet. According to dog websites, eating poop is quite common among most breeds but this habit can be stopped with preventable measures especially for a puppy. One website assures that eating poop is natural for dogs, not a mental illness. Good to hear that...

0 Likes, 15 Comments

------*there is an enzyme you can buy for that, I believe it is a pill.*

------*Scooping the poop is important in so many ways!*

------*but then the geese come around and it's like a party in itself!*

------*then they roll in it!*

------*(From Lisa Rapacki the dog trainer) what food are you feeding both dogs? make sure no corn, wheat, or soy. especially corn, it comes out the same way it goes in, just like us. you can also try grated zucchini mixed in with both dogs food.*

------*Bainey, put red pepper on it!*

------*Try hot sauce*

------*cayenne pepper..*

------*Try putting pinapple juice in her food. Makes the poop taste more like poop instead of a tasty treat for her. We have to watch Scooby like a hawk WHILE he is pooping, or he will turn around right away and eat it. We put pinapple juice in his food to make the poop less tasty. Don't know why it works, but it does. We haven't noticed it bothering his little bum though. What's gross is he licks his lips as he poops.*

------*I have never had a dog that did that. I don't even think that I've heard of that.*

------*I have seen dogs eat cat poop...*

------*(Bainy comments) My yellow lab Olive, who passed away four years ago, constantly ate my cat's poop, although she was well fed. I wish I'd known about the meat tenderizer or hot pepper or pineapple juice back then...*

------*we have the same problem here with one of our dogs....let me know if you find a remedy.*

------*why bother putting hot pepper on the poop while you could scoop them up right away, but dashing their food with it? OW the bottom hole will throb for sure! Lol*

------ought to try the pineapple juice as long it's good for them! :)

November 7

Thanks to many of you for your helpful suggestions on how to fix coprophagia (dog eating poop). I'd rather start on the food than mess with the poop so I've got zucchini and pineapple on hand since they make very unappetizing poop. And I also have this brand new poop bite in order to pick up every single one I can find in the yard. I know I'll beat this nasty dog condition. Della and Mabel, here come your zucchini pineapple entrees!

2 Likes, 3 Comments

------ I actually heard of one trick I haven't tried yet that is supposed to work. Add Meat Tenderizer to the dog's food and it makes the poop unappetizing. I kid you not. Haven't tried it yet but need to. Daisy and Riddick the Westies think that Captain's poop is their favorite delicacy. it is DISGUSTING beyond words. We have to take Captain on a separate walk to do his business so Daisy and Riddick aren't tempted. so gross it makes me shudder.

------let me know how it works out for you. we have two poop-eaters! Makes yard clean up easy, but is SO nasty!!

November 8

Please excuse me if I continue posting about dogs eating poop and I promise this will be the last one. Just in case you have dogs with the same problem and want to fix it. Well, I think I've got it. When I took Della out for a walk tonight, she went about her business no less than eight feet away from me and my gosh, her excrement laden with pineapple juice stank to high heaven. It was just pungent. So you see why the pineapple poop can be unappetizing to dogs. Yes, pineapple juice mixed with dog food is the remedy so far. I haven't had a chance to slice and blanch zucchini yet but will. Maybe the smell will be even worse. Please forgive me, neighbors.

1 Like, 6 Comments

------ *when I'm ready for my next dog, I am going to call on you for any and all questions!*

------*(From Cousin David Kabler the dog trainer) Also, she may be eating a diet that is too rich. Some of the foods are so rich that much of it goes undigested. I personally feed a small amount of iams supplemented with whole food table scraps. Most people over feed their dogs, although proper nutrition is extremely important in puppy development. If nothing else works ya'll should give me a call for a phone training consultation. I've enjoyed seeing the pics of your dog Della!*

------ *First, the poop eating-thing is often a puppy thing. Second - if she is eating her own poop - feed her pumpkin - it's supposed to make their own poop taste bad (again, who figured that out?) And bitter-green apple or tabasco is a great deterrent!!!!*

------ *Congratulations on conquering the problem. I threw in the towel on that one a long time ago. Dog poop, kitty poop, elk and coyote poop; it's all good to the dogs and so readily available that the best I can do is look away.*

November 9

Uh, Della, don't you know chairs are for sitting down?

Photo Taken at Happy Tails (Della's collar and chair are red)

7 Likes, 6 Comments

------ *She's adorable!*

------ *But Mom, I match the chair!!!*

------ *Waiting for her Merlot!!! :)*

------ *So pretty!*

------ *You need to frame that picture ! Seriously !*

------ *Della's picture is great and her collar matches the chair!*

November 11

Done with a three-mile walk with Della. With a big puppy you cannot saunter. No, not powerwalking. I mean, racewalking. There has to be a difference between those two!

1 Like, 1 Comment

------*Yes, Bainy. Leash training. LOL*

November 11

A true Lab...

24 Likes, 11 Comments

------ *My son has been in that spot many times and the water as well. All sea creatures are at risk when the net is out!*

------ *"anything you need me to fetch, momma?" :)*

------ *What a great picture!*

------ *Love it Bainy. Makes me miss Harvey!*

------ *Beautiful picture!!!*

------ *pretty sweet!*

------ *she is so dog......*

------ *♥*

------ *awww..that's so cute...hard not to love her !! :)*

------ *I dog sit a beautiful high energy Yellow Lab named Nixon for a Naval Officer whenever she has to deploy. He is the smartest and most playful and well behaved dog I have ever met! He will fetch and return until it wears ME out! Amazing dog...no leash required when we are out because he's always at my side "on the job"!*

------ *wow! beautiful!*

November 12

We figured out something about Della last night: She is not a wine lover like our other yellow lab Olive (pictured) who drooled over port wine at only four months old and enjoyed red wine all her life and even drank her last glass of Cabernet at almost age 13 - an hour before being put down due to an age-related ailment. Anyway, we tried with Della, first giving her a teaspoon of Cabernet and then port. She sniffed, winced, and crawled backward into her grate. So we'll have to give her cranberry juice instead...

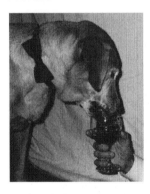

1 Like, 7 Comments

------*love the bow :) makes her look sophisticated*

------*Port! I want to be a part of the next test session*

------*Bainy, I think Della is a Beer kinda girl....just saying.*

------*Try giving her a sweeter wine. Apollo likes jack/coke!*

------*Nice try on trying to calm Della down. Sorry it did not work!*

------*More wine for you two!!!! ":)*

------*HA!*

November 14

Happy Monday! Della had an appetizing breakfast this morning. She picked a cockroach right off the kitchen floor and chomped it down. Approved because a bug is more fortified than a BM.

1 Like, 7 Comments

------*(From Bainy's brother Harvey) Bainy, if you write one more doo-doo dispatch about your dog's bowels, I'm going to hurl.*

------*I am with Harvey on this one*

------*(Bainy replies) Grin...last one, I promise.*

------*Bainy, how did you like growing up with three older brothers?*

------*(Bainy replies) Harvey is the worst but I still love him.*

------*Bainy, Keep them coming. I think it is funny as BM :)*

------*hope the caca doesn't crawl*

November 16

Doesn't Della ever have enough to eat???

3 Likes, 3 Comments

------Our Lab does the exact same thing!

------I think a stainless steel feeding dish might be in order

------Wouldn't you wonder if it wasn't clean?

November 17

You can recycle a dog bed even after 4 1/2 years. I let Della wander around the house under my watchful eye and she laid down on Mabel's huge round bed. So I thought it was time to pull out Olive's similar bed from the garage and pass it down to Della. The bed is about 75% clean but just dusted and vacuumed. Olive's smell seems to linger there and Della already likes this ghost bed. Maybe she will eventually learn to like wine...

2 Likes, 1 Comment

------we just put an old bed in Hazel's crate- she ripped it to shreds. Guess it was too early for her!

November 19

As we're heading to Florida for a week, the house is being taken care of by a friend and the two dogs are at separate kennels. Mabel is at a senior spa where she can sleep all day without interruption and Della is at a Pre-K spa with the dog trainer and four other dogs where she can play all day without interruption...

3 Likes, 3 Comments

------now you just announced to the world that your house is safe to party. What's the address? (3 Likes)

------Maybe she has a strong alarm system...

------*(Bainy replies) Stephanie is right. Not only that but also a beefy bar bouncer.*

November 21

Down here at the Tampa RV Resort with senior citizens. Never seen so many Chihuahuas and other toy-sized breed dogs sitting or napping on the big dashboards inside the RVs, most with fluffy pillows. I don't think it'd be a bad idea to put Della and Mabel there on the dashboard whenever we take them on an RV trip...

0 Likes, 1 Comment

------*Reggie is usually hanging over the windshield in my convertible. he loves the wind!*

November 24 (Thanksgiving Day)

Lisa the dogsitter (and trainer) sent me this picture of Della all decked out in feathers!

Photo Taken by Lisa Rapacki at her house

11 Likes, 5 Comments

------*Aw... she misses you & your husband, Steve but she will do fine.. :-)*

------*This is THE best dog...*

------*Snoozin too.*

------*Aw, cute!*

------*Great Photo!*

November 27

It's good to be back home from Florida. Steve just took Della to Dunkin Donuts in his little pick-up truck to get pumpkin donuts, possibly the last of the season. The clerk at the drive-thru apologized for running out of dog biscuits but offered a donut hole or "munchkin". Of course, Della snapped it up. I'm afraid she'll eventually develop a sweet tooth...

3 Likes, 0 Comments

November 27

Della tore apart my custom-made wine cork wreath that I had paid a lot of money for. Corks, fake grapes, silk leaves, and straw all over the kitchen floor...Maybe she's starting to develop a taste for Cabernet Sauvignon like our old Olive?

2 Likes, 7 Comments

------*oh no...hope della not eat*

------*Della is in the dog house.*

------*Della, bad dog!*

------*Not nearly as bad as when our dog- years ago- climbed up on the dining room table and grabbed the meat off of the platter that was to be served for dinner. Meat gone- toenail marks still on the table!!! A fun(?) memory of a great dog named "Happy". Every time I see those marks I think of her and what a fun dog she was. RIP "Happy".*

------*OH no! Soon she is going to make you think you made a mistake in giving her a good home. 8-(*

------*It is never a mistake to open your home...it is only material stuff...Della is precious!*

------*All the things my dogs have destroyed have been replaced...but I could never replace what those dogs have given me :)*

November 29

Soon to put up a Christmas tree. Has anyone heard of dog-repellent ornaments? I think I'll invent a few today.

1 Like, 14 Comments

-----*(Bainy adds) Maybe a "bitter apple" with cloves all over it. That'd make a pretty ornament...*

------*anything with tabasco sauce will keep her away.*

------*(Bainy replies) So maybe a red pepper with a green bow would look nice?*

------*apple? I dont think so! that's Bella's favorite fruit eh how about dried pineapple turds?*

------*It's called a smaller tree on a table.....similar to a toddler-repellent tree.*

------*You can borrow our white picket fence we made 7 years ago when we brought two puppies home on December 17, 2004. And I decorated the white picket fence with garlands, lights, etc. Really darling, and it all worked out just great!*

------*Animals don't like moth balls. Too bad it smells bad to humans too.*

------*Huh no tree in the house Mary Pat? ;) That's why I decorated the tree with unbreakable ornaments! Sure I had several trees falling down, but NOT the dogs' fault, it's the cats!*

------*Patty, we had the tree up with glass ornaments, then put the white picket fence around the tree. Worked out just perfectly.*

------*My daughter has a one and a half year old (human), so she is painting a tree on her window this year. Lila won't be eating any ornaments that way!*

------*Bitter Apple may help!*

------*I did the bitter apple thing when Pepper was a puppy!!! Worked like a charm!!! Now the cat.... she's too clever for me! Have to tie the tree to the wall every year now!*

------*Oh a picket fence around the indoor tree? Lol good idea!*

------*Sounds like bitter apple works, but with what or just let them rotten?*

December 1

What's even more awakening than coffee is when you come down to the kitchen and be knocked down by a nearly full-grown puppy who then puts its arms around your neck and gives you a big sloppy kiss on the face. I don't need any more coffee...

8 Likes, 4 Comments

------True love, indeed! Next time be sure to wear protective gear!

------yup you just need to be taller :)

------Nothing beats a still soft puppy's fur and its soft licking tongue with lessen sharp teeth this time of their age! ain't they?!

------Still they melt our hearts no matter what kind of morning or evening whenever they came to greet us, right?? :)

December 2

Dogs seem to have an appetite for paper. Della just pulled down my 15-year-old carefully typed list of phone numbers and devoured it. No bother because that list had only house phone numbers which have not been used in nearly a decade. These days dogs can't eat cellphone numbers because we store them in our phones instead of making an old-fashioned list and taping it to the side of the refrigerator. But for extra caution, keep your cell phones out of reach...

3 Likes, 2 Comments

------And your remote control to the flatscreen TV!

------Sunshine likes to eat books. If she's bored while I'm at work she just takes one off the shelf, tears off the cover and binding and spreads the pages all over the house. I can't even begin to count how many books she's destroyed in her 8 years. I think they like the sound of the paper.

December 2

Della at Happy Tails today. Photo taken and captioned by Jana: "Watch me. When I hold my legs like this, my ears stand up, too."

25 Likes, 12 Comments

------*Oh thats cool yeah watch me !!!*

------*"And I look like a reindeer! Mommy will like this."*

------*Love the kangaroo imitation!*

------*oh, hahahahahaha!!!!*

------*I can't tell if the other dogs are saying "awesome" or "who let her in?" hahaha*

------*No problems!! I know YOU Just LOVE him!!!! Busy Busy Puppy!!! Hopefully he will grow up!! :))*

------*(Bainy replies) It's a SHE, Keith!!! Lady Gaga!!!*

------*(Keith replies) Who cares he or she! ha Our Poodle is a Tomboy!!!! :)*

December 2

More on Della...I had bought her a red Christmas collar adorned with Christmas trees accompanied by a silver jingle bell at the buckle. Well, she came home from daycare missing the bell. Steve expressed worry that Della had eaten it. I don't think so because he would've heard the bell in her stomach. So far, no jingles...

2 Likes, 0 Comments

December 3

Okay, I've made a decision when it comes to a six-month-old puppy about two feet tall: Decorate less Christmas stuff. No glass ornaments, no Dickens Village houses, no poinsettias, no trains, no breakable or edible things. Now, proceed.

6 Likes, 7 Comments

------*We put all the breakable stuff in the dining room and living room, Christmas tree with breakables is in the front foyer and we look at it through the class French doors...dog and grandkid proof!*

------*By George, I think she's got it!*

------*Bainy, one year we went all out and made an edible gingerbread train with 250 small cookie cars that circled our dining room table. I came downstairs to find Dexter had eaten close to 218 of the cars and was laying on the kitchen floor unable to stand from the weight of his belly.......ugh....*

------*Good luck to della monday.....big girl day. (Spaying surgery that day)*

------*Bainy, I should also add that he chewed the wire off of 9 Christmas reindeer in our yard......I found copper wire in the yard for months after:)*

------*Exactly why we are waiting til after Christmas to get a new puppy!!! I'll never forget the first year with Pepper--- ended up having to tie the tree to the wall with fishing line!!! :-) She gave us a great 14 & 1/2 years though!*

------just hang a bell on the doorknob and Della will provide music for the holidays!

December 4

I'm not looking forward to Della's required rest with no Happy Tails daycare for TEN days, beginning tomorrow after her spaying. How can you calm a puppy especially with a lampshade collar? Your suggestions would be much appreciated but I do not plan to give Della Valium, thank you.

1 Like, 5 Comments

------I have had a lot of dogs spayed/neutered, and although the spaying is considered to be major surgery, in my experience the dog feels fine 24-48 hrs later. The fast recovery makes it nearly impossible to truly keep them quiet. I do try to enforce no jumping or hard running, but beyond that I haven't had much luck and thankfully have never had a post surgery complication. Go to the butcher at your grocery store and get some good marrow bones - keep the extras in your freezer. They are great for all around good health and will also serve as a quiet distraction during recovery. PS - Not all dogs need the E-Collar. Give Della breaks from it while you're there to watch her. You might find that she doesn't chew/lick at her stitches at all.

------After having gone through this with mine many times I would suggest 4 things :) Large "BUSY" bones or frozen filled Kong's to occupy her mind; An inflatable collar versus the cone version for comfort and its harder for them to "outsmart" ;) ... Third to control her when she's walked so she doesn't get away, run and tear her stitche,s I would only leash walk her with a " Haltie" or other head collar in place; and lastly I would consider

pain meds in addition to the shot they recieve during surgery (which wears off rather quickly) at least for day one following surgery.... Not to calm her but to make her more comfortable and manage her pain... Imagine if it was us? ;) Good luck Della and Momma Bainy ♥

------Bainy, YOU take the Valium. It always seems so ridiculous when they send mom and puppy home and say "keep her calm, no running and jumping!"...uh-huh...now HOW in the world do you do that? And the cone of shame...with all 4 of our dogs that have been spayed/neutered over the years, I took it right off because they are sooo pitiful and can't even get to their water bowl. But...you need to do what the vet says! :)

------Our 7mo. old horse (goldendoodle) was neutered recently and the "cone of shame" stressed him out so much he developed colitis. Trip to the vet, a few antibiotics and removal of the cone shaped him right up. Good luck Bainy!

------Jake bothered his stitches BAD, but I would take the collar off and give him a break whenever I could sit with him.

December 4

Della on top of the tree!

5 Likes, 3 Comments

------How???

------Aaaw, that is neat...

------If you can't change her, join her...

December 5

Just had Della spayed and microchipped.
No babies or missing dog flyers (hope the second will work...)

5 Likes, 1 Comment

------ahhh, sleep little Della!

December 5

Della doesn't know why she keeps bumping into things while she has on a clear lampshade collar - and it breaks my heart to see her miserable and drugged out of her mind but that won't last long. Hopefully, she'll be back to herself in the morning and eat some...

1 Like, 0 Comments

December 7

Minus her ovaries, Della is back to herself, feisty and hungry as ever. It's not easy to tell her she can't run or jump for the next seven days. At least she doesn't bother her stitches and that ridiculous Elizabethan collar is rarely used except for bedtime. She even tried to eat it. I don't blame her. So I'd call that collar "The Cone of Revenge".

3 Likes, 0 Comments

December 8

**RIP: My favorite reading glasses.
Cause of Death: Malicious wounding with severe bites and missing parts.**

8 Likes, 6 Comments

-----*She was getting you back for the ovary thing...*

------*DELLA!*

------*I bet Della said, "There you go!"*

------*Hey Bainy, my sister Susie's dachshunds ate both of her hearing aids!*

------NOTE...... the smell of the ear molds (ear wax). All dogs ATTACK them.

------Mom woke up one morning with her toy pom chewing on Mom's dentures...apparently her dog thought she might be able to eat better with more teeth, lol

December 8

The post-surgical rule - no activity for ten days - is driving a bored puppy nuts. And it is driving its owner nuts, too.

2 Likes, 2 Comments

------This too shall pass...

------Just think if she were a child and could cry, whine, talk, throw temper tantrums.....you have it easy. LOL

December 11

I've got two house members here fighting for peanut butter: Steve and Della. No wonder one jar runs out quickly. So I need to buy two at a time. Steve likes peanut butter on his bread and Della likes it inside her real marrow bone so which is more appetizing???

2 Likes, 1 Comment

------Steve's bread!

December 12

Well, alas, I cannot finish the book I've been reading because Della tore it into pieces. But I'm grateful it was only a paperback, not a Kindle...

4 Likes, 6 Comments

------*What book? Maybe one of us has it.*

------*You can help me, Bainy. I just got an audio book for my Kindle. What do I do now?*

------*oh my goodness......*

------*do you crate her when you leave the house?*

------*Sunshine loves to eat books, when she feels neglected she takes them right of the bookshelf . First she tears the binding and then pulls all the pages out.*

------*I say better if it were a kindle, except that the toxins in the kindle would probably seriously harm her.*

December 12

Oh geez...Della just managed to reach a bunch of bananas far off in the back of the counter while I was in the office. She ate 2 1/2 bananas and some of the peels. I checked the website to see if bananas are safe for dogs. Well, yes, they are but will result in "very loose bowels." Wonderful...And I swear Della let out a huge burp.

2 Likes, 10 Comments

------*Uhh, I hope there's no "accidents" in the house. Once, I cooked dinner and put it on the kitchen table and turned around to wash dishes, my lab got on top of the table and ate everything in less than 5 mins then puked. Needless to say, he was in the dog house for a while.*

------We once had an old hound dog named Big Buddy who loved bananas. Seemed no matter where we put them he'd find them and frequently ate a whole bunch only leaving the very top where they all connect. We started calling him Banana Buddy. He also ate light bulbs, children's Tylenol (went to the emergency vet late at night for that one) and an array of other things.

------With a dog who eats everything, perhaps you should start keeping Hydrogen Peroxide handy (to induce vomiting when necessary), as well as the number for animal poison control. Also, familiarize yourself with the signs of bloat, (we once went to the vet with two bloated labs who together ate a 40 bag of dog food). We have had two other dogs suffer from bloat/gastric torsion for no apparent reason. It's a scary thing!

------(From Nora the breeder) Eating books, jumping on the counters, eating the bananas. Della is turning out to be a bad juvenile delinquent. She is taking advantage of you. I feel so bad! 8-(

------(Bainy replies) But Nora, she is no Marley. I just love her to death. :-)

------Bananas are Lily's favorite treat!

------They will not hurt her, but peels YUCK, I have a dog I know that eats bananas for its treats. No leg cramps fro him!!!

------my girls eat a banana most days, you shouldn't have any problems.

------My dog eats banana's with me all the time. He's too short to get up on the counter but I have experienced that before. My golden liked used cooking utensils, so we got them from the $ Tree. Got to love em

December 13

Another emergency visit for Della: She got into something in the back yard while I was gone for a few hours and her face was swollen, eyes shut and itchy. The vet said it could be an allergy to a certain plant or a spider bite. Della seemed fine, even grabbing a biscuit, and had no temperature but her face was three times bigger. She is now at the vet for a few more hours and I'll have to give her Benadryl at home. Have any of you had a similar experience with your dog(s)? I looked around the yard and didn't find anything unusual but noticed a piece of pittosporum pulled out and chewed. But that plant is not toxic, according to the website. Any idea???

1 Like, 14 Comments

------*I had this happen once with my German shepherd when I was living in Miami. He had bit a frog. face was HUGE!*

------*Oh my goodness Bainy. With 3 dogs and a landscaper's yard full of plants year round, I have never had that problem. Maybe a frog like Janita mentioned. Hope she heals quickly.*

------*I'm thinking bee sting or something like that. I know it is cold out but I have seen an occasional bee here and there. Worked at the dog and cat hospital for ten years.......seen a lot of the swollen faces before!!!!*

------*wasp nest was the culprit when this happened to our puppy.*

------*My basset used to get into a wasp nest and the stings would do that. Careful care.*

------*You should get a secret boyfriend with a vet practice, Bainy.*

------*Bee sting!*

------*bee sting and a frog---Lily has run into both!!*

------*Dexter had a huge swollen face from a large bumble bee sting....very scarey as it affected part of his mouth but luckily no posterior swelling which would have altered his ability to take a breath. I had a child this week who was stung several times by a mud wasp even though the temperatures have dipped. Possibly a sting?*

------*The other thing that was helpful was an antibiotic powder that healed lesions my Basset got into.*

------*Ground Bees...happened to a Lab that I dog walked...I arrived to his face looking like Alfe the alien...he had gotten into them in the morning and when I arrived his face and nose was swollen so much...I was off to the Vet with him. Benedryl is all they did for him. It was normal the next day.*

------*Hope your pup is feeling better*

------*Hope Della is better. I think about bees.*

------*hi Bainy....my dog, Snicker, was bitten by a snake when she was a puppy and her face was huge....they gave her an antibiotic injection.....it took a few days....so sorry about Della*

December 13

Her face is slowly contracting...What a day. Since I believe it was the culprit, I'm going to have to find a wasp nest...

2 Likes, 19 Comments

------*Poor Baby.*

------*ohhh poor puppy! This happened to Daisy and Riddick. they bit a bad frog!*

------*Oh my goodness! Better add Benadryl to your arsenal, too. This wonderful pup is definitely keeping you on your toes!!*

------*Might be a wasp or hornet bite.*

------*Might be the bananas from the kitchen counter. LOL!*

------*Bainy, as mischievous as Della is, you may want to get pet insurance!*

------*Same thing happened to Peanut when she was a pup...hope Della's feeling better!*

------*Benadryl is Della's friend. Same thing happened to our dog and vet said just give her Benadryl - who knew!*

------*She still looks beautiful*

------*Maybe someone told her about SANTA PAWS...she has worry bumps!*

------*oh no poor Della, hope the swell goes down this morning. My Bella got a pink eye last night that we rushed to the vet when her eye rolls back, it sure scared me! And the vet confirmed that she has conjunctivitis like us having pink eye, poor Bella, too :/*

December 13

Okay, I have a theory about Della's elephant face: It was either a wasp or hornet.
Fact 1: There is obviously no nest in the fenced back yard.
Fact 2: Frogs appear to be in hibernation at this time of the year.
Fact 3: There are no toxic plants on the ground that the owner knows of.
Conclusion: Della chased a wasp or hornet and was stung several times on the face.
Puppies certainly learn the hard way, don't they?

0 Likes, 6 Comments

-----*I agree...*

------*I thought I had posted this, but maybe I didn't: My dog had the same thing happen she caught a bumblebee.*

------*Our first dogs would catch and eat flies. One day she ate a bee and one side of her face swelled up!*

------*I remember learning the same thing as a kid.*

------*We have a hole full of beelike creatures in our yard and there is one at the Hermitage. You may also have one in your yard. They can be dangerous.*

------*Poor puppy! Watch out for bees!*

December 13

From today's comments on my posts about Della's bee-stung swollen face, I wonder why we humans don't ever have our faces blown up from bites by bees, frogs, or snakes. I guess we should feel lucky that God created hands for us and snouts for dogs, just for exploring and touching. No wonder dogs will never get into beauty contests...

0 Likes, 6 Comments

------Lots of people do get very swollen from bee and wasp stings. And guess what instantly takes away the pain? Taking some tobacco, like out of a cigarette, wet it and press it on the sting...hurty is gone in seconds.

------...unless you are my husband----swells up like a blowfish.......

------I guess if we got stung on the face, we would swell up there. Dogs use their noses for hands in a way. I've also heard a sliced onion pressed against a sting calms it down too.

------Yeah, humans don't really go face first into a hornets nest. LOL.

------Only metaphorically Chrissy, only metaphorically :)

------LOL, Grace!!!!!

December 15

Fully recovered from a bee sting allergy, Della killed my little Christmas cactus with nice pink blooms I brought home from a party last night and stupidly left on the counter before taking the other dog Mabel for a walk. When I came back, the kitchen floor was black with dirt. That prompted me to have another glass of wine and haul a vacuum cleaner...

3 Likes, 13 Comments

------Oh s---

------Is Della okay with the needles? Oops!

------Aww! :-(I've had mornings like yours. Hope Della didn't get hurt and hope things are looking up for you soon.

------(Bainy replies) She's fine. A Christmas cactus is flimsy and harmless. It's not like a porcupine...

------LOL Glad you had that wine available. Sounds like you'd better stock up on that, too!

------She's just keeping you young and on your toes.

------You need to write a new book about adventures with Della! ;)

------(From the party host) I'll bring you another one!

------We got home from a trip to Charlotte and our 8 yr old Layla managed to eat a loaf of bread....she looked guilty too! Guess the crate is coming back out.

------Captain Destructo struck again, did she? LOL Got to love having puppy energy in the house! :)

December 16

There's always something going on with Della. But it can happen to other puppies and dogs as well: plant poisoning. Della threw up twice today after eating a few parts of lantana, a flowering low shrub. As a former horticulturist, I figured it was the lantana and looked it up on the website and yes, it is one of the toxic plants for dogs. So I removed three lantanas from my yard. And the castor bean is the worst, even fatal, so thank goodness I don't have that. Della is just fine, still robust and hungry. That dog has got a lot to learn.

0 Likes, 11 Comments

------*Omg....at least nothing super horrible yet. Glad she is okay.*

------*My dog got into something once like that, they gave her atropine which worked quite well.*

------*Glad she's okay Bainy but I'm thinking she needs to be watched a little closer, at least til she's past her puppy stage. Trust me, been there with Bear, lol He's 3 and still wants to consume a lot of what comes into his sniffer and eyes.*

------*Juniper berries are not great for dogs either*

------*Jazz ate lantana too! She was sick, sick, sick!*

------*omg....this dog is giving you more heart ache that you deserve!!!!*

------*Lantana. Oleander. Chocolate. Grapes. Lots of stuff that do not belong in dog's belly!*

------*Watch out for mistletoe berries that fall from overhead, too.*

------*be careful about coconut liners too. Sunshine got into that one time and had eventually had to have her entire intestinal track taken out and the vet had to clean it out by hand. Needless to say it was very scary and expensive.*

------*Watch your medicines. Skyler got my pill box off the counter and ate 2 of my pills yesterday morning.*

------*winter daphne is also fatal. I had to put it in the front yard not the back after I found that out.*

December 16

Great Gift from Nora the breeder!

7 Likes, 3 Comments

------*At first glance I thought Della had a new earpiece for her "doggie" cellphone.*

------*me too :) She is too cute*

------*Cute!*

December 16

Della got her spaying stitches removed, finally. Cold, metal ones. Last week two people, who are dog pros, incredulously asked why her stitches were so long over her belly, about four inches instead of a normal two inches. I didn't know the answer but assumed Della had big eggs!

2 Likes, 0 Comments

December 18

Unfortunately, Della was born into the world of multitasking. She doesn't seem to know how to play with one ball at a time. She wouldn't let me take the tennis ball from her mouth while demanding that I kick the old basketball across the yard for her to run after. Then she would try to pick up the teaser ball even with the tennis ball still seized in her mouth. Three balls at the same time...Kinda scary because dogs can someday metamorphose into humans who have developed a terrible habit of multitasking.

1 Like, 0 Comments

December 19

Never carry a cup of coffee in front of a big puppy. Gotta clean up the mess. Happy Monday, anyway.

4 Likes, 3 Comments

------*Ha! Ha! Ha!*

------*you are sure learning alot from that pup....isnt is supposed to be the other way around?*

------*Me thinks that puppy needs to play outside ;)*

December 20

Knock on wood...Della has not made any more emergency visits to the vet in the past seven days. Let's hold our breath until I take her back there for her October 2012 Bordetella shot.

5 Likes, 2 Comments

------DON'T JINX IT BAINY!!!! "Della the Explorer" - I want a signed copy!!! :-)

------You need to take that back, you are jinxed now.

December 22

Della smells like daycare, dirt, grass, rawhide, dog food, dirty bed, and whatever is not very refreshing to the nose. So she is getting a Christmas bath!

4 Likes, 3 Comments

------Same here!

------Mango just got her "hair done" this week. Nothing could be cuter with plaid bows in her hair!

------I hope that you have a red Christmas hat to go with Della's Christmas bath.

December 24

Well, doggonit...I bought Della a Christmas present: A Kong rubber frisbee which I thought was unchewable and indestructible. That red rubber was thick and flexible. I tried to teach Della that a frisbee was for throwing but she ran around with it and wouldn't let me pry it from her mouth. So then she went on eating three inches of the edge before I gave up and threw her Christmas present away. She might as well eat a car tire. Anyway, Merry Christmas...

6 Likes, 7 Comments

------I don't know who has more energy...Della or Bainy. Keep the story coming! You ought to write a book titled "Me and Della"! Merry Christmas to you all!

------You have to admit that's pretty funny Bainy :). We are due for lunch in the New Year ;).

------Goodyear makes many types..... I feel the same way as mine chews up the woodwork in the kitchen.

------Guess what Bainy? She's gonna make fast work of a car tire too. Merry Christmas.

------And our Bella unwrapped our presents while we were sleeping this morning, aint that great, all these work wrapping them with love and tender care! lol Merry Christmas :) P.S. Oh I like this Kong's pear shape to tease the dogs with treats inside it, I already knew that frisbee isn't the right choice anyway!

December 25

Merry Christmas! Here is my brother Harvey's gift for Della and Mabel. A great way to keep those dogs out of the bathroom!

19 Likes, 5 Comments

------cute

------love it.

------Really?

------LOVE IT!!!

------(Bainy's brother Harvey comments) the tagline on the box said "When you're tired of waiting for your dog to get out of the bathroom!" I was sold. Merry Christmas B & S..

December 26

Della is doing a little better with sitting and half-gently taking a treat from my hand without biting it off. But I certainly don't appreciate a huge glob of saliva on my palm.

3 Likes, 1 Comment

------Thump her nose when she starts to take it too hard.

December 27

Della turns seven months old today so is that the beginning of the Pre-K phase???

5 Likes, 4 Comments

------ha ha that is at 6 years old....

------Closer to the teenage phase - yikes!

------She's a lab...so yes, she is six!

------*With a lab, at least two years of puppy. If you both make it that long, you'll have a great dog. Our labs went from puppy to adult, seemingly overnight.*

December 28

OMG - I just saw Della through the window dancing around something in the back yard and she appeared overexcited. I knew it was some animal she was trying to get so I ran outside. Della managed to grab a struggling rat into her mouth. But I scared her away and picked up the limping rat in a scooper dooper and threw it outside the fence. Urgh...Della is still looking for it...

3 Likes, 9 Comments

------*So much for Kibbles & Bit's!*

------*oh no didn't she know that she s a dog not a cat! lol poor dat rat :/*

------*I wonder what your neighbor will think about you putting the rat over the fence!!! LOL!!!*

------*Not sure I'd want her to kiss me right now....:-)*

------*Hope she had her rabies shot !*

------*(Bainy replies) Della is vaccinated. Rat is fine. But owner is shaken.*

------*lol...I was saving a rat from my Jack Russell and cat one day*

------*Do not have to worry about rabies and if the dog is properly vaccinated you do not have to worry about anything else but the rat poison it may have inside it. I had a dog who killed a rat, the vet told me no worries unless he bit the intestines open as a rat can have enough poison in it to kill a dog - my dog was 80 lbs.*

------Our dog is the master mole chaser/killer ... she has gotten 2 this month !! At least moles are cuter than rats ....

December 28

So far I haven't seen any dead rats since I caught Della with one in her mouth this morning and saved the poor struggling creature's life. It's always nerve-racking coming home and not knowing what to expect in the back yard after leaving Della there most of the day. The only evidence of Della's mischief during her owner's absence today is a small piece of tarp that has been shredded into confetti - which she had yanked from the top of a firewood pile. God knows what will happen tomorrow when I work way out in Newport News? An overturned patio table? An uprooted shrub? I guess it'd be better than a dead rat...

4 Likes, 4 Comments

------No, rats are best dead! I hate rodents, they are gross!

------Well I have a shrew running around in my house somewhere, BW brought it in yesterday and lord knows where it is now.

------That's why I stay home as a housewife all over again since our three grown kids left. Because of our puppy Bella, my husband wants me staying at home since Bella is still a very mouthy and impossible pup. I enjoy having her around cause she'd be a worthy hearing guidance dog to us someday hopefully sooner than we think :)

------careful she doesn't dig under the fence and escape while you are gone (that is what my dogs did!)

December 29

Young kids and puppies do have something in common: An attachment to a favorite stuffed animal. When I bought Della this pink stuffed bear (or whatever it is) last month, I was concerned she'd immediately tear it into pieces but she never did. See how much she loves it. Della also puts it in her mouth for comfort.

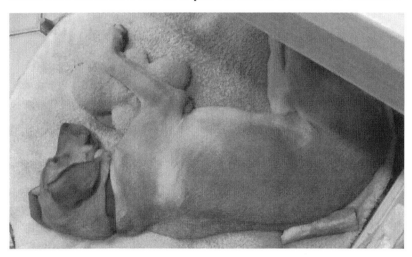

26 Likes, 8 Comments

------*Snuggle buddies.*

------*precious dog...*

------*Aww...her "lovie"*

------*Layla had a Christmas toy last year that lasted 9 months before it she killed it!*

------*our dog Aussie used to call her Wally! She would go get it when we told her to get Wally. Love those dogs and their pets!*

------*Sunshine had a soft stuffed ball. Della is so adorable!!*

December 30

Came home to find snow on our backyard despite this beautiful warm day. I mean, it was the shredded styrofoam box Della had pulled from the overloaded garbage bin.

4 Likes, 6 Comments

------*yea we found pink thingy shredded all over our living room that I forgot to put away my fluffy pink old slippers, ahh great, but I need new slippers anyway!*

------*Dogs are sweet and special and just like having a toddler in the throes of 'terrible two' for a very long time! Good luck!*

------*That doggie is VERY busy! !*

------*She was just helping decorate some! She missed all the snow last year and must have heard about from one of your neighbors dogs. She just wanted to play! Haha!!!*

------*Bainy I look forward to hearing about Della on a Daily basis. She is so puppy love it!! Keep the stories coming...*

------*You should keep a log book and then write her story,,,"Della & Me"*

January 2, 2012 (New Year!)

We're slowly letting Della walk loose in the house. So far, so good. No chewed shoes, broken lamps, or jumped furniture. Only under our watchful eyes...

2 Likes, 3 Comments

------*you being watchful? i don't think so, you're obviously facebooking! HEH*

------*you never let her loose in the house since she was a puppy??*

------(Bainy replies) For heaven's sake, Della is STILL a puppy!

January 3

Took Della for a three-mile powerwalk in the freezing cold but it was nice under the sun. Della needs to learn that blowing leaves are not critters as she keeps chasing them down the street...

5 Likes, 0 Comments

January 3 (Later in the evening)

So here we have got snow flurries. They are frightening Della as she doesn't know what the heck they are. She's now trying to bite them.

5 Likes, 2 Comments

------ Bainy, I love your posts about Della! :)

------ If Della is anything like Bailiff was, by the time she's got it all figured out, she won't be a dog, she'll be a person ♥

January 4

Yes, Della, you can come to the dishwasher when it's dirty but not when it's clean...

3 Likes, 3 Comments

------ She's the Best Dishwasher! No Germs!!! ;)

------ and with their keen noses they do know the difference. But beware of dogs putting their feet on the door when it's laying open. Mine did that and threw our new dishwasher off balance, so now it's not working properly.

------ Zeus loves the dishwasher.. when he was small he would climb on the door (i know a bad thing) and now that e is huge it doesn't work. he loves to clean dishes.. what a mandog...

January 5

Aside from my posts on Della, I know I haven't mentioned Mabel often here but there isn't much to tell about a centenarian mutt who has gone completely deaf and half blind. But in the past few weeks Mabel has started to play some with her housemate 14.5 years her junior. I swear she RAN, not hobbled, with Della after the ball yesterday about five times. It was something she hadn't done in a while. Don't they make Geritol for dogs???

6 Likes, 4 Comments

------ Awwwww !!!!!!!

------ I love the dear, sweet senior dogs; they're filled with so much heart and soul!

------ My Susie follows me EVERYWHERE. We are best friends.

------ George's dad gives his dog that glucosamine chondroitin stuff. he swears by it!

January 5

Still laughing after a quick visit to the vet. I went solo to ask if I could buy an eyedrop for Della since her eyes turn red every now and then. The assistant at the front desk, who I've known for years, regretted that she cannot sell any type of medication unless I see a vet and suggested making an appointment. I began telling her that Steve and I had done research and believed that

Della has a common eye condition called conjunctivitis. The assistant cut me off in annoyance and wailed, "Stay off the Internet!"....

3 Likes, 5 Comments

------ That's awful!! Why cannot people just use common sense instead of follow the letter of the rules so rigidly that they negate good will!!

------(Bainy reassures) That assistant was just playing with me, not 100% serious. I can understand why vets are cautious about prescribing medication before seeing their patients so I am okay with taking Della there tomorrow - just to be safe.

------ Oh. Good! But it seems like eye or ear drops or flea stuff wouldn't necessitate a full exam. Honestly does everyone want more or what!!

------ That's hilarious!!

------ Bainy, just get a boric acid solution at the drug store - it is cheap and works for humans and canines!

January 6

The vet weighed Della this morning and she is now regrettably unliftable as a Michelin baby - all of 60.2 pounds and many more to come. I really miss the days when I could lift Della with one hand...

3 Likes, 3 Comments

------ One-hander puppies don't get in nearly as much trouble

------ Our 8mo old Doodle just weighed in @ 67! I need to send pic. He's huge.

------ Hi Bainy, just had my almost 8 year old dog (golden retriever) weighed at the vet. Exactly same as Della!

January 7

I wonder if dogs can actually show body language to convey their thoughts and feelings. Della is not too thrilled about having her eyes applied with eye drop. I swear when this morning I pulled out a small white bottle, she knew...and started rubbing her eyes and burying her head in the bed. She even made a face. But she allowed Steve to hold her up for me to apply the eye drop. I plan to videotape the next time if Della does her amazing action again.

1 Like, 9 Comments

------ Rosie does the same at eye drop time

------ Get the book, "Canine Body Language A photographic Guide" by Brenda Aloff (Amazon has it); you'll love it!

------ oh they know alright!! We had to start giving Hutch his flea/heartworm meds by pill b/c when i would get out the advantix he would run & hide, its hard holding down a 100lb beast while trying to apply the meds carefully...lol!! Della is a RIOT, i love hearing all of your stories Bainey :)

------ When Bailiff was in the house and wanted to go for a walk, he'd come nudge me. If I said, "you want to go for a walk?" his ears would pop up and he'd get all excited. Lot's od dogs learn that, no big deal. But, I could say, go get your leash, and he'd run to the kitchen and get the leash off the back door and bring it to me. Well, lots of dogs can learn that too. But, sometimes if I didn't respond to his hints, he would bring me one of my shoes, and drop it at my feet. And if I told him, "go get the other one" He would run off and return with the other matching shoe to that pair of my shoes. Now that was remarkable because we were a family of 8, and

114

my shoes were never left in the same place! He could get the right shoes for everybody else too!

------ @ david: must have been the smell..... Well, dogs are real good with smells ya know, to be able to tell although different shoes apart.........♥

------(David replies) we mountain men like to call that a "scent" ...as a way to give credit to the dog, as opposed to attaching a stench to its best friend :)

------ Bailiff was also known for sitting and looking both ways before crossing Hampton Boulevard at Baldwin Ave. What was unique was he did it when he was loose, on his own in the neighborhood.

------ But this is about Della, she just reminds me of a great dog, because she is one. Thank you Bainy!

January 8

Della actually went swimming for the first time, eagerly going after the stick we threw into the semi-shallow water in Lochhaven. As a true Lab, she didn't care about the freezing temperature. We had tried the ocean last summer but it was too rough every time. So I cannot wait until we take Della to the beach when the surf is calm. Maybe even in the wintertime, since she may not even know the difference between the room and arctic temperatures!

3 Likes, 1 Comment

------come to Willoughby, the surf is calm and there are dogs to play with. My goldens swim most everyday.

January 8

Getting big...

22 Likes, 10 Comments

------*This is the most precious dog.....*

------*Cute BiG Puppy!!!! ;)*

------*she has great expressions*

------*All legs and paws. She must be a good swimmer. She is getting big!*

------*She is growing up! Love all her adventures!*

January 9

A startling loud "AAAAH!!!" can really work with a mischievous puppy. Seems to be more effective than "NO!!!"

0 Likes, 4 Comments

------*I say that often here, too. Also, although I don't agree with everything Cesar teaches, I've found his quiet "ch" sound to be amazingly effective.*

------*I say "ehhh" and if that doesn't work she gets a "NO" and then a quick squirt of water/listerine (water/listerine recipe a great tip from my friend. Doesn't hurt but she doesn't like it. Nothing else worked, not Cesar's hand thing or "ch" or anything else. I tried it all!*

------*For my cat, "Ah-ah-ah!" very high pitch voice.. she hates it, but it works.*

------*My pup thinks her name is NO! NO is a friendly name gesture to her till I said hey that's EEenough! with my pointing finger at her face and she barks right back at me cause she hates that word!*

January 9

After picking up Della at daycare, I stopped at Kroger's and bought a half-week's supply of food. I felt very smart throwing bags of canned food, produce, and laundry detergent in the back seat - and placing only one bag in the front seat with me - as far as from Della in the cargo area. What was in that bag? A steaming rotisserie chicken. Della had even thought of climbing over two seats to get her snack but several "AAAAH!"s stopped her.

6 Likes, 2 Comments

------*I love your dog!!!*

-------*I was wondering how long that bag would last you!*

January 10

What is so appealing about Kleenex, multi-purpose copy paper, and even toilet paper? Della goes after every one of them, chews them, spits them out, and goes out for some more. She yanks a Kleenex from the box, a copy paper from my office trash can, and unrolls the toilet paper. No wonder every floor in this house looks like it's been plastered with paper mache.

1 Like, 7 Comments

------*I think I remember hearing it's the glue in paper....at least she is spitting it out! :)*

------*Bainy, Bainy, Bainy...that is THE most novel way to blame the innocent little puppy for poor housekeeping skills that I have ever heard!*

------*(From Nora the breeder) Della's brother got caught dragging the toliet paper roll thru the house, and it was still connected to the bathroom wall. She sent me pictures of him getting caught! 8-)*

------*(From Nora the breeder) Mahala, I think you might be on to something....When Bailey, Della's mom, was a puppy she loved tape. Especially duck tape, and we had to hide newspaper from her because she would tear it to shreds.*

------*Fond memories of our golden retrievers and miniature poodles!!!*

------*Sunshine likes paper products too. When she was a puppy she liked toilet paper and the newspaper but then she discovered books. She takes them off the bookshelf tears off the binding and scatters the pages all over the house.*

------*After seeing you and Della out for a walk, She looked so sweet that I find it hard to believe. However, she is still a puppy!*

January 12

OMG...Della is already a teenager and thinks she is Kid Rock. Help, I need your parental advice on how to handle this rebellious kid...

(Photo taken and doctored by Jana of Happy Tails)

12 Likes, 4 Comments

------*Hahahaha I love it. that pic is awesome, amen.*

------*any tattoos yet??*

------*Lady Gaga !*

------*All she needs now is toe nail polish on those long toes!*

January 13 (Friday the 13th...)

Here's what Steve said after finding the plastic cover on the grass and returning it to the cable box: Della got tired of the poor TV program so she chewed the wires. But no damage to our cable. Large trash bin now blocking the wires. If you want to chew Cox Cable again, Della, chew the trash can first. Good luck.

0 Likes, 6 Comments

------*There goes the trash can!!*

------*ditto what Stephanie said. Remember the indestructible frisbee?*

------*Bainy...put some hot sauce on the trash can where Della might start to chew and she should stay away from it...just make sure she has water around to drink.*

-----*(Bainy replies) But that city-owned trash can is as big as a bulldozer with the plastic as thick as a bulletproof window. Definitely dog-proof.*

------*we will be waiting to hear :)*

------*it has been our experience that NOTHING is totally dog proof once the dog decides to mess with it*

January 13

Another destruction in the Cyrus household...Della managed to climb up on the patio bench and pull down an old rusty RV birdhouse where wrens, chickadees, and finches had raised their babies all these years. Now it's uninhabitable, chewed to pieces. But thank God birds don't mate in January. Before spring the birdhouse will be rebuilt and hung much higher.

5 Likes, 6 Comments

------*Just never a dull minute with Della....LOL*

------*Are you sure her name isn't Marley!*

------*I think you should have called her Georgie... as in "curious george"'. Della is one very busy dog.*

------*Oh my goodness Bainy you have GOT to start writing that book, lol*

------*are you sure she's not a boy?*

------*Can we do a write-in campaign for Della for President? Maybe she could chew up Washington.*

January 13

Della attacked three things on this Friday the 13th: birdhouse, patio pillow, and cable wires. Is this really bad luck? We've got 6.5 hours to go and I'm getting nervous. Anyone got a black cat I can borrow to scare Della away from any more destruction?

0 Likes, 3 Comments

------*Muzzle? Mice traps on anything edible?*

------*Maybe u should try walking her while you are riding a bike! Tire that girl out!*

------*geez I think it's time for you to make a specific area with a trolley leash for her to be unreachable mouthy place! So you can save your pretty landscaping back or front yard :) That's what we did, and it sure works.*

January 15

When I see that one of my shoes is missing, then I know who did it.

7 Likes, 13 Comments

------*yeah, and they always go for the most expensive or favorite pair!*

------*now, now, now . . . don't go jumping to conclusions!*

------*Bailey got Matthew's shoes yesterday too! Now need to get him another pair. They were destroyed. Many times I have told him to put them away.....He might listen next time?????*

------*This morning my 6 year old golden had my hat and both gloves along with some toys surrounding him as he napped. Fortunately, he's old enough that he doesn't chew them up any more, but he still loves my stuff!*

------*Dogs teach you to put things away. We have to hide our bread!*

------*I wonder who?????*

------*Della!*

------*lol my Bella ruined my husband's new slippers for christmas, man why do they love our smelling feet, eh?*

------*Naughty Steve.*

------*I had a german shepherd who was VERY well behaved. If you had done something to make him angry, he would take one of your shoes and put in the middle of the living room floor. Untouched, just sitting there. My husband or I would come home and it would be (insert singsongy voice here) "OOOOO what did you do to Mac?...you're in trouble"*

------*wasn't me!*

------*Susie used to go into my closet and get one shoe and take it outside through her dogdoor. I would wake up and have to go out into the yard to retrieve my shoe. She never really did any damage to them, just her way of saying that she didn't like it when I left her alone!!!*

------Carolyn, that is too funny, I think it was kind of a "If I was a bad dog and left alone, look what I could have done to your defenseless shoes"

January 16

Home Builders: If you're building for a family with a big dog, make the kitchen countertop four feet high, not three. Della got my cereal this morning.

8 Likes, 8 Comments

------Don't know if I should "like" this remark or not!!

------and Bella got my last piece of toast! lol grr

------She'll get it all at the higher height too. . .from experience!

------Always a daily adventure with Della. I think she is more adventurous than my two boys when they were a year apart as babies and toddlers. You are such a patient momma.

------I've heard these dogs can be trained not to do that....but I've never seen it proved to be totally successful.

------How many more gray hairs have you gotten since Della arrived? :)

------(Bainy replies) Too many, Carina.

------I don't believe the countertop height is the problem here....

January 16

Reading Glasses Number Three Gone. Side Frame Missing and One Len Cracked. Thank God I had LASIK four years ago. THREE destroyed PRESCRIPTION glasses would have sent me to the poor house.

2 Likes, 0 Comments

January 17

When I arrived at a friend's house this evening, her Jack Russell terrier started sniffing my feet and legs with intensity. He wouldn't stop and followed me around and continued sniffing me right up to my hind. So there, you see I had Della's perfume on me...

0 Likes, 5 Comments

------ *We used to have a Jack Russell. . .finally had to put her down. She was WILD!*

------*Kevin used to love the fact that our beloved "Pepper" 'goosed" my mom every time she came into the house!!! Haha!!! I guess there are some ways you can get your frustrations out on your mother-in-law with very little effort!!! :-)*

------*Then when you go home, Della will smell the Jack Russell terrier.*

------*Haha Molly!!! It's a vicious cycle now!!! However... this leaves tons of room for Bainy's hilarious "Della Tales!!!"(I want the first copy of the book Bainy!!!!)*

------*(From the Jack Russell terrier owner) Spencer, my Jack, says he wants Della to come visit!!! :)*

January 18

Photo taken and captioned by Jana of Happy Tails
"Don't sneak up on me like that...you scared the tennis ball right
out of me!"

14 Likes, 3 Comments

------*That is so funny!*

------*hahahahaha! cute!*

------*She'd make a great barrel racer. Look at that turn! Hehehe*

January 18

Dogs seem to go after the same particular thing. Here I was
affectionately massaging Della's head and she suddenly lunged at
the top of my head. She wanted my reading glasses and we
fought over them on the sofa. I managed to grab my glasses out
of her reach. Now I'm not certain about leaving my reading
glasses on top of my head if I ever lean over to Della. No, no.
Number Four can NOT go.

3 Likes, 7 Comments

------so it's not that she just goes after things when she's bored! .....
maybe a bad sign.

------You need Dog Whisperer...

------(Bainy replies) Overall, Della is a good puppy, not like Marley, but she
definitely has a taste for reading glasses.

------Maybe needs them to read something on the dog food label?

------lol at Neal...my Bella has a thing for my hearing aid!! Now I couldn't
find it since yesterday and I wondered!

------Izzy thinks that some part of our morning walk should always include
a period of biting my legs and playing tug of war with my pants. Glad I
have good balance.

------Our first dog had an iron stomach. Ate 2 pair of glasses and thought
my underwear was a delicacy. Wouldn't know she had eaten the panties
until she pooped them out......whole.

January 19

**Why can't Della learn to drink water gently instead of lapping it
up with voraciousness and leaving a trail of puddles as she walks
away? I'm seriously thinking about buying a "Wet" sign in case I
have guests to ensure their safety...**

2 Likes, 2 Comments

------I've got 2 that do the same. Have wiped out several times from the
puddles. :(

------My 2 do the same thing. I mop up several times a day...

January 19

Oh geez, not again. We took the big garbage bin out on the street today after it had been guarding the cable box from Della. Guess what? She got it again this afternoon, yanking the cover off and chewing the wires just like last week. We'll need to find a way to guard the box, maybe find a metal cover and bolt it into the brick wall? Anyway, I wouldn't be surprised when she gets older and chases the Cox Cable truck off our street.

0 Likes, 5 Comments

------She is just trying to spare you all of the bad tv on cable!!

------She needs counseling.......... ....LOL

------Maybe there is something emitting a high frequency sound from it?

------You crack me up! Sounds like me ranting on FB about my boys and their friends! You definitely have your hands full with Della! I have a 2-year-old white lab named Marley (after Bob Marley, mind you) and I think we jinxed ourselves when we got Marley around the same time the movie Marley and Me came out. I feel your pain. Hang in there, Mama. This too shall pass. :-)

------(Bainy replies) I am okay with it. At least a puppy keeps me young! :-)

January 20

Peeking out to see who's coming home...

22 Likes, 3 Comments

------Angel and I went to Happy Tails last Fri afternoon, we just missed you all.

------That is TOO CUTE !!!

------What a face!

January 21

The Cox Cable is coming today to repair what Della had done...

6 Likes, 5 Comments

------lol.......Isn't that precious :)

------Dexter ate every single external cable around my entire house.....plus chewed on the outdoor outlets......had to get boxes to cover them.

------you should make a book about all her antics--one day she will be old and you will actually wish for these days.

------you should try Direct Satellite TV...don't think Della can reach the roof!!!

------Is she crate trained? Puppies left to their own devices.....well, you know!

January 23

Della, be nice! (At Happy Tails)

3 Likes, 3 Comments

------her tail does not look so happy. maybe they should rename it "crazy fangs"

------Mango must have heard of Della's antics. She chewed up one of my hats and found a bag in the closet with shoe products and ate that too!

------She looks like a vampire bat!

January 27

What's that tune???
(At Happy Tails today)

6 Likes, 1 Comment

------really really loved and read your Della's personality and stuff going on here cause she just keep reminding of my Bella a few weeks younger than yours :) Always loved seeing your pup's pictures from time to time here ♥ We ought to get together with our ( )ELLA pups! someday soon! :) xx

January 27

Florida has been heaven with great friends, laughter, beach walks, bike rides, sunsets, and fish tacos. But I look forward to coming home to Della and Mabel who have managed well with Linda the house sitter. Thanks, Linda, for keeping Della away from the cable...

3 Likes, 1 Comment

------OMG! FISH TACOS!!!!!! I am glad you had a good time.

January 28

Can only one week of your absence tell you whether your puppy has grown bigger or taller??? I can't quite tell the difference in Della but her tail seems to have increased in speed...

6 Likes, 0 Comments

January 29

We came home yesterday from Florida to find a new dogbone tag on Della's collar. There is a story behind it. Last July Larry Burge the neighbor kept Della for a day in secrecy before Steve gave her to me at my birthday party. Throughout that day Steve had checked in a few times on this feisty little puppy tearing up things in Larry's yard and kept saying the same thing over and over. Well, this new tag, given by Larry, says "What was I thinking..."

8 Likes, 0 Comments

January 30

Rubber Ducky is gone. Head torn off this morning. No real duck for Della. And no hunting either.

3 Likes, 1 Comment

------when Kevin was 2 he had a plastic recorder that he would walk around with playing the same note over and over. One day I was gardening and found it buried...clearly the german shepherd had heard enough....

January 31

Hmph...Della took my chair.

15 Likes, 14 Comments

------*looking for those pens i bet....*

------*and she looks quite handsome there!*

------*If she starts typing on your laptop, make sure you get that on video! :)*

------*Look at my timeline and see the golden retriever listening to music and you'll know when it stops because of his hysterical expressions....enjoy!*

------*lol wow she's big!*

------*Does she type and answer the phone, too???!!!*

------*Della is a beautiful dog and cute to sit in your chair...*

------*I have a sexy little ginger dog that would be a good secretary. They would have fun playing. She's a wild woman and loves to run if she ever needs a playmate.*

------*Is Della looking at the cable box outside?*

January 31

Good Grief! Getting an early start on Halloween...

8 Likes, 8 Comments

------*what in the world is she up to?*

------*What a spirited pup!*

------*are you sure Della's not related to Marley? (4 Likes)*

------*Nothing like puppy mischief! So cute!*

------*This dog is hysterical.....*

------*Actually, Karen, our golden must be related to Marley....*

------*She is just taking a break...from digging!! love it!!*

------*Too funny!!!*

February 1

My garden, which was once on the tour, has become misaligned with little figurines relocated into one place, PVC pipes and firewood scattered around, a beheaded concrete turtle lying in grass, fishpond rocks thrown into water, an overturned birdbath and no flowers. Hey, Garden Club ladies, would you consider my garden again for the tour this year???

12 Likes, 6 Comments

------*Let me guess, Della? Lol*

------*Sounds like Gnomeo and Juliet are at it again!*

------*LOL!*

------*The difference between a garden and a habitat is livestock/pets!*

------*Dogs don't make good landscapers in case you hadn't noticed.*

------*Maybe Della needs a canine playmate. Two dogs keep each other happy playing together like my Lucy & Desi. They don't tear up the yard as long as they and run and play "chase me".*

February 1

I think Della has ADHD.

9 Likes, 11 Comments

------*Another Dog Happily Deranged?*

-------*Hey, remember that she is only a puppy and will stay that way for 2-3 years. Then she will start to settle down. Don't worry your pretty head off!*

------*I remember when I used to say that about Sallie. :D*

------*Lol my kids finally grew up after being 21 years old so naturally I knew that it d happen with my Bella just like yer Della, too. Lmao, didn't you know dat?!*

------*Ha, ha, ha, ha!*

------*(From Jana the owner of Happy Tails) Della is part ninja too. She launched an ambush and ate my bagel while I was taking a bite. I don't think I have ever heard Jessie (co-worker) laugh so hard.*

------*Desmond has 'selective" ADD*

------*(Bainy replies) Sorry, Jana.*

------*(Jana responds) Good grief, do NOT say sorry.... I am in the dog business and clearly I do not need the calories of a bagel. We laughed so much over this one.*

------*Don't you think that Bainy and her hubby just spoil their Della? :) :X*

------*just decided?*

February 1

Do they make Ritalin for dogs?

0 Likes, 11 Comments

------*Actually, they do! I had a friend in DC who gave her dog ADD meds per a vet prescription!!*

------*Haha*

------*yep, they do!*

------*She'll grow out of it Bainy!*

------*She's a lab!!! She'll grow out of it when she's five!*

------Our golden pup just turned 1 year old last week and he can't concentrate on anything for more than a few minutes. I bet raising twins would be easier!

------Embrace the puppiness. It will be gone before you know it..

------Love that..."Embrace the puppiness"....got to pass that on to my daughter who just got a very active border collley puppy.

------Bainy: Not to worry, she'll settle down when she's seven or eight. :-)

------I have a three year old Rottie. Just told my husband tonight I wish I could have just a couple of days with him when I got him at 10 weeks old. Nothing like a rottie puppy.

------Doggie Downers....nice!

February 2

On the way to daycare this morning Della tried to eat my box of business cards but I managed to yank it out of her mouth. I don't think my boss would be pleased if Della ate the cards.

2 Likes, 2 Comments

------awwww......

------Maybe you need to order her own cards...

February 3

To the bank drive-thru, thank you for my money and a dog biscuit.

3 Likes, 2 Comments

------Do you remember when they used to give us lollipops with the little twisty thing instead of a stick?

------When I was working at Crestar Bank (a long time ago), they tried cutting out the dog biscuits as a cost saving measure. It was hilarious how many letters the senior management team got protesting the change. Many of the letters were supposedly written by the dogs themselves and some were signed with paw prints. They reversed the decision quickly!

February 3

When I went to pick up Della at Happy Tails this afternoon, Jana the owner told me that it had been so crazy with dogs fighting because of the full moon. I'd never heard of that so I researched on the Internet and learned that dogs and cats do get into mischief during certain phases of lunar cycle when the moon is at its fullest. And there is an increase in emergency visits to the vet. No wonder where that word "lunatic" comes from. Uh oh, I'll have to keep Della from doing crazy things in the next few days. She already chewed off one leg of my kitchen stool...

3 Likes, 0 Comments

February 4

Della, tomorrow is Super Bowl. Don't you dare, I repeat DARE, get into the cable box.

10 Likes, 3 Comments

------Holding good thoughts!!!!!!!

------Might need a neighbor's house for back up.

------Good luck Bainy!

February 6

(Referring to the Super Bowl ad with Huff the Great Dane challenging his owner with Doritos to keep quiet about the missing cat)

Della cannot bribe me with Doritos because I don't have a cat.

5 Likes, 4 Comments

------*But the neighbors do!*

------*But you have cable ;)*

------*Is that a great dog or what??*

------*I love the commercial!*

February 6

Della...where did you hide your dog bowl in the yard? Without it, you won't have any supper. Better bring it back to me.

1 Like, 1 Comment

------*Does Della have a FB account?*

February 7

I never say "Hello" to Della when I come home.
Instead I always ask, "So, what have you done?"

13 Likes, 2 Comments

------*That hurts her feelings you know. She senses you don't completely trust her, Bainy*

------*(Bainy replies) Who can ever trust a puppy???*

February 8

Because of the full moon at its peak, Della was restless last night as she refused to sleep by the fire. Instead she tried to get on poor old Mabel's nerves, jump on Steve's lap in his leather recliner, grab my iPad, eat a Forbes magazine on the coffee table, and even stick her head right into the fire. Geez, if the moon is full again tonight, I am going to put Della on a desert with coyotes so she can do no damage and howl along with them.

3 Likes, 8 Comments

------*Della needs a crate where she can feel cozy and in control! My two cents.*

------*Della needs to come spend the night with Libby, They can be crazy heads together.*

------*I'll send Desmond over and they can tire each other out!*

------*she's a beautiful baby who is growing up to be a very bad girl. My kinda gurl :)*

------*(Bainy replies) Della does have a crate and sleeps in there only at night. And she also has another bed in the corner and sleeps there in the daytime and before bedtime. But we sometimes move the bed to the den by the fire for our evening gatherings.*

------*Please keep up the Della updates here, I like them.*

-------*Hey Bainy, maybe her crate needs to be redecorated. She is a teenager. Maybe a pink Princess phone??*

------*LOL she sure reminds me of my Bella, but that's their job to drive us crazy anyway, well especially the pups! ha ;) Hey have you read Cesar Millan's new book "Be the Pack Leader"? It's awesome and very resourceful that I read it overnight before the holidays, and plan to reread it in concentration when I'm on a vacation to FLA next month :)*

February 9

I had to chase Della with my bra in her mouth but fortunately she didn't get out of the house. That would have been a huge embarrassment. So you didn't see nuthin'.

11 Likes, 11 Comments

------*lol, Bear loves underwear and socks*

------*lol one time Bella brought out my underwear to show and tell with a friend who visited us and it was hilarious and embarrassing, too. :) funny*

------*LOL that's funny. It is full moon today. My cat acts little wild this morning.*

------*My dog goes for tampons and pads. Yuck. How embarrassing when you go in a room and find it shredded everywhere with company visiting.*

------*hahaha*

------*Desmond's favorite item... he trolls my daughter's room just waiting for the opportunity...*

------*Has Della seen you chasing Steve around the house with your bra in his mouth? Just wondering how she learned that trick! LOL*

------*Branigan loves my bras too!*

------*Who gets the Doritos? You or Della?*

------*Crazy dog.*

------*The day I saw you walking Della, she looked like the perfect lady.*

------*(Bainy replies) Perfect lady? Sometimes.*

February 10

So here I came down after a morning shower and putting on a freshly laundered white shirt. And made a dumb mistake of letting in the dogs for a morning greeting. Della sprang up to me, placing her wet paws on my shirt. It was before I realized she had once again buried her face and paws into the muddy fishpond. Shirt back into the washer...

1 Like, 4 Comments

------*You continually make me laugh with Della stories!*

------*been there! ugh... hahaha Stock up on Clorox ;)*

------*Bainy, you are too funny. I love reading your post about Della!*

------*Bainy, after numerous experiences like yours , I started wearing "dog clothes" in the house. Have to be able to withstand doggie love! When I get dressed to go out, I make sure the dogs are in their crates or outside. Love my dogs, but not on my clothes.*

February 10

Imagine the worst case scenario: Your dog tears up a check made out to you and then you have to call the payer and explain the need for a new check - or even give up and lose your money. Della almost got my book royalty check and instead ate the envelope.

0 Likes, 11 Comments

------*lol.... two words... "direct deposit" ;)*

------*Hey Bainy - I once threw away a tax refund check. At least she only ate the envelope. Have you ever tried to get a duplicate check out of the IRS?*

------*Bainy, I had a friend house sitting one summer. She brought in the mail which included four new boxes of checks......Dex ate them allllllll!*

------*Why isn't she crated during the day? Lots of people do it. Not sure how it works... I have cats so no clue....*

------*Della's version of the dog ate my homework!*

------*I was a branch manager at banks 20+ years.... Happens all the time! hahaha ;)*

------*(Bainy replies) Cindy, we wouldn't want to keep Della in her grate all the time during the day because she needs to learn the surroundings both in and out. And it's good for her to explore as long as we keep things out of her reach.*

------*(Cindy replies) I am not sure how others do it, seemed a little mean to me, but.... I wouldn't want to be in a crate all day, BUT she has destroyed a lot of your stuff lately, or ran off with "things", lol She might hurt herself too, eating something she and have to have it surgically removed.*

------*this has happened to me more than once. never put your check in the same pocket you put treats.*

------*Bainy: You know, there is always obedience school!*

------*Watch out for when the tax return checks come in. Rusty ate part of the envelope last year!*

February 11

Now that I know how to type a heart from the keyboard, I'm going out to get a heart-shaped rawhide for young voracious Della and a heart-shaped biscuit for old teethless Mabel. (I just learned that you need to type < and 3 without a space to get a heart symbol.)

3 Likes, 0 Comments

February 11

Weatherman, I thought you said it was going to snow here in drearily dull Norfolk. I'm anxiously awaiting Della's first snow.

1 Like, 3 Comments

------*yeah thats big exciting for Della ...*

------*Give it time! It just got to Mechanicsville:)*

------*(Bainy later comments) We ended up with only a dusting of snow but it created enough curiosity for Della this morning as she came out, became a little spooked with the white grass, prodded it with her paws, ran back and forth in perplexity, and then prodded the grass again. She didn't know what the heck it was.*

February 12

What to do with an eight-and-half-month-old feisty Lab on a freezing day? Steve took Della out to the Meadowbrook park and ran her hard with a ball along with 15 other dogs including a humongous, big-headed black Lab and two yellow ones. Now I see why owners take their restless dogs to a park when it's 32 degrees - to wear 'em out!

2 Likes, 2 Comments

------*Works every time. I could always tell when my dogs were finally exhausted, their third eyelid starts to partially close and they get this thick wrinkle along their cheeks under their eyes. That's when you know they're totally whooped. Saw it every time.*

------*Oh yes I always took my Bella and Princess out for a walk around my 7 acres homestead every morning walks to wear them out so I could do my chores all afternoon! It worked like a charm except for rainy days they sure got very restless indoors! Lol*

February 13

Della has begun to understand English language. She suddenly freezes and stares at me, her big Labrador ears straightening into the shape of "Yield" signs and her mouth clamped shut...whenever I ask "Do you want supper?"

3 Likes, 0 Comments

February 14

Della has roses for you. Will you be her Valentine? (Photo taken at Happy Tails)

37 Likes, 10 Comments

------Absolutely!

------*She's gonna eat 'em!*

------*THANK YOU DELLA !!!!!!! HUGS TO YOU TOO !!!!!!!!!!*

------*Sweet! Did she dig those out of your garden? LOL!*

February 15

Good morning! I've made a decision. I'm going to enter Della in the next year's Westminster Kennel dog show. Will need to find a catwalk for her to practice so she would walk right...

2 Likes, 4 Comments

------*I love dogs but didn't the best in show look like a square wooly worm? Talk about your bad hair days, get that dog some conditioner.*

------*dogwalk?*

------*(Bainy replies) Whatever. :-)*

------*She's a sho-in to win*

February 16

Puppies 101: Always, always keep ballpoint pens out of reach. I was lucky to grab one from Della before she turned the inside of my car into a Pollock painting.

1 Like, 1 Comment

------*My lil Bella seemed to think that her name is Oh No no, maybe I should just change her name to Ono!*

February 17

It rained hard last night. That's why I plan to wear dog clothes today. Black pants with unseen paw prints and a windbreaker with wipeable paw prints.

1 Like, 0 Comments

February 17

Friday Night Crash...

21 Likes, 8 Comments

------*Steve, hello, are you there...*

------*It's a dog's life :)*

------*Too much Mexican Food?*

------*All worn out and time for zzzzz*

------*Familiar sight... looks like Della is taking over*

February 19

Picture a 50-year-old woman roughhousing on the kitchen floor with an almost full-grown Lab puppy for a half hour - while there is nothing to do outside in the freezing rain...It helps to keep young but not become a magnet for dog hair. Now I even have brassy yellow highlights in my graying hair.

8 Likes, 6 Comments

------*Does Della have the puppy zoomies? Izzy runs laps around the room and tries to grab the remote control. I think she wants to watch Animal Planet. I'm covered in white hair today...it matches my gray.*

------*and u didn't have to pay for them. I was out playing with my pup today. The things we do for our babies :)*

------*I like to wear a black sweatshirt just for fun when i do that.*

------*That was a fun visualization. Thanks! I needed a good giggle.*

------*what's age got to do with it!!!*

------*oh yeah I can picture you wrestling with her!*

February 19

Oh swell...Della just ate six small tomatoes from a plastic bag she grabbed off the kitchen counter. And I'd just fed her a big supper. I assume she remembered all the tasty tomatoes she pulled off Steve's vines when she was a tiny little thing...

1 Like, 5 Comments

------*shes gonna be pooping out ketchup!*

------*Maybe she just wanted a salad!?!?!?!?*

------*or needed licopene*

------*Oh no, but be aware that tomatoes can cause dogs vomiting or muscle tremors or stiffness if they had so much. It said so in my book about golden retrievers, but I don't know about other kind of dogs?? Hope your tomatoes were all organic thou. :)*

------*(Bainy replies) It's been four hours since she ate all the tomatoes. So far, no sign of distress. Still a robust puppy but now in bed for the night.*

February 20

Della, no. You can't bring a four-foot-long tree limb into the house.

6 Likes, 8 Comments

------*Hee hee, we can relate. Happens often here. Lol*

------*here too*

------*..and sand covered rocks!?*

------*Don't you love it? They swing those damn things and obliterate everything within a four foot radius.*

------*(From Nora the breeder) She definitely got that from her momma!*

------Ohhh, why NOT, mommy!!! Come on!!

February 20

Oh gosh...there it goes again...when I came down into the kitchen after a shower, Della was laying down on her bed which had red spots all over. And her mouth had some red in there. It was my lipstick.

3 Likes, 11 Comments

------OMG

------Eeew. She ate your lipstick.

------just proves she's a girl.

------(From Nora the breeder) Getting ready for her doggy day care boyfriends tomorrow!

-------unless she's still teething, it doesn't make a lot of sense that she wants to eat...everything...My cousin had a lab that had a kind of disorder, that he ate socks, just swallowed them whole, and then he'd have to get operated on sometimes. I hope that's not the case with Della. With my lab, we never stopped him from getting to food if we left it unattended, but he never ate things that weren't food. Keep an eye on that...good luck!

------(Bainy replies) Della seems to enjoy having a cloth napkin or dish towel in her mouth but never eats them so I guess she's OK.

------Bainy, you have got to write a book about that dog! ;) I'd buy it!

------Bainy, I know I should not laugh, but this is very funny to me.....my Dex was EXACTLY like this!! So wonderful and so very naughty......

------I have had many labs....this one has more personality than all combined...........and I love my doggies!!

------*Oh my gosh with Della all the drama.*

------*lol at Nora!*

February 21

Despite a heavy wash in hot soapy water, Della's bed is still stained with my lipstick. Well, the heck with it. At least Della has got the girly decor...

1 Like, 3 Comments

------*Have you tried Goo Gone? If I remember correctly it removes bizarre things like crayons and lipstick.*

------*? She stole your lipstick? Lol bet she wanted to be just like her pretty mommy, too!*

------*:o{}*

February 21

Since it was on the same counter with my now-defunct lipstick, I felt I had to save my old amplified house phone from Della and therefore removed it from the kitchen but not far because the phone plugger is above the counter. So...I taped the cord upward on the wall away from the plugger and around the open door and on the dining room wall and back down to the phone sitting on the high stool. And stuck my tongue at Della.

3 Likes, 3 Comments

------*You're a trip.*

------*Elly ate my new prescription glasses :(*

------*but still your "dinosaur" home phone is still within Della's reach, so you better hang its cord away from her, too!*

February 21

On a serious note, it's a shame when you hear of a dog hit and killed by a car as it happened today. Of all these years I've owned dogs, I tend to be overprotective during every dogwalk even on quiet, empty roads like those in my neighborhood. It's because I cannot hear a car coming. Steve once thought I worried too much but then realized that there is indeed an advantage of being deaf when owning a pet: You use your eyes to protect and prevent an accident for your pet. That's why I hold onto the leash and look around for cars even in an open area such as a parking lot. So Della will always be safe with me. :-)

20 Likes, 4 Comments

------same here girl, we're here to protect our babies......

------Bainey you are an amazing person!

------what dog??

------Amen!

February 23

Della, don't be chicken. Get in the pool!
(At Happy Tails today)

16 Likes, 6 Comments

------But them crazy heads, Libby and Desmond are in her way!

------(Bainy replies) Three Yellow Lab Musketeers!

February 23

**Yea! You finally got into the pool!
(At Happy Tails today)**

6 Likes, 2 Comments

------*Nice shot*

------*She's beautiful!*

February 24

I learned a lesson: Never mind mopping the kitchen floor when it is 80 degrees or higher outside. Della has acquired the same cooling maneuver our other Lab Olive had invented: Play hard, get hot, take a dip in the fish pond, submerge oneself up to the chest, stand there for a few minutes, climb out, and then wait by the side door. As soon as I open the door, not knowing what she has done, Della barges in and tracks mud all over the floor. Put away the mop. It will happen again today...

2 Likes, 1 Comment

------life with labs is fun and they definitely teach us to have a sense of humor.

February 26

I just realized Della will turn nine months old tomorrow. By calculation, she would have been 5.25 years old as a human. I think it's time for Della to have an imaginary friend. Scooby Doo? Astro? Deputy Dawg? Snoopy? Goofy? Uh, how about Garfield???

4 Likes, 3 Comments

------I think Dinky would be good for her. Do you remember that cartoon? The end of the theme song, "No Dinky No!"

------lol

------In dog beers I've only had one.

February 28

(Steve and I are vacationing at Disneyworld's Fort Wilderness for a week where we first learn to use Segways around this campground. I have just posted a picture of us on those machines earlier on Facebook)

As you saw the earlier photo of me and Steve on the Segways for the first time, these machines are pretty easy to operate but I do not recommend dogwalking with a Segway. Della would've left me flipped upside down in a ditch.

0 Likes, 4 Comments

------Yes!!!

------and she would have eaten a wheel or something....

------you do know the guy that designed them died riding one off a cliff?!?!

------I thought she does that without a Segway

February 29

Some dogs like this one can go so far as to try to eat a house. Della would probably try but cannot eat a brick house. So we're safe. (This unknown picture was posted on Facebook by an animal organization and it was obviously viral so I did not need permission to repeat this post.)

7 Likes, 12 Comments

------oh no ... Aww Della is cute :)

------(Bainy replies) That's not Della. Someone posted it and I had to repeat. Thank God, not my dog.

------You need to contact The Dog Whisperer....I'd love to see you and your dog on that show! I love Ceasar Milan!! I don't even have a dog and I have been watching his show for years.

------she is bored!

------(Bainy replies) Again, this is not Della. She doesn't need Dog Whisperer yet!

------Don't be so sure. My Golden likes to chew rocks.

------Layla ate 3 of 4 cupcakes today. Paper wrapper and all....

------Oh geez, Kim...labs eat anything, don't they?

------When I get my new Samsung Galaxy, I will definitely take a picture of the torn drywall that my doggies did! There was a squirrel running around in the crawlspace, and my doggies got so excited and tore the drywall up!!!

March 3

Looking forward to picking up Della at the kennel tomorrow. It's been a long eight days without excitement of puppy life. I need to get back into the anti-aging process...

2 Likes, 0 Comments

March 4

Della is back home after spending nine days at the Sterling Meadows Kennel way out in the horse country and the staff there stated that she had a blast the whole time as I was shown a brief video of her playing tag with other dogs on the pasture. At least Della was bathed and perfumed for her homecoming. She also slept and napped on the Kuranda bed offered at the kennel as you see the below picture. I wonder if any of you ever use this type of bed for your dog(s)? Although Della has a fluffy bed and was delighted to see it upon her arrival home, I am thinking about buying a Kuranda bed for our RV travel since it is easy to clean. Pros or Cons?

3 Likes, 10 Comments

------*I heard the bed is great for pups. I looked into purchasing 2 for my babies. pricing is deceasing as well. if you purchase let me know how della likes it..*

------*Lily has one. She loves it, and it is easier on her joints as she ages.*

------*Bet Della didn't miss you while she was being pampered there! LOL Just remember that our dogs have such a short and very forgiving memory that no matter how long you were gone, they forgive you and love you all to pieces.*

------*I have one of these beds for my dog, Sammy; he would rather be on the bed, but my neighbor's dog and my friend's dog love it. Very well made, would recommend.*

------*You can make it yourself with PVC pipe and fittings - sailcloth w/ velcro would be washable!*

------*I think it is a great idea, however, Brogan would eat it, no doubt!*

------*I guess Della was good and didn't try to eat the kennel. I guess your house tastes better to her!!!!!!!*

------*Alot of folks on the lab owners forums have them and like them*

------*I have an Orvis dog bed for our labs and it's a hit. They claim the cover (not cheap) is chew proof. It is. At least for my two wild things!*

------*Our lab Zamboni has one. Would recommend*

March 5

When I went to the bank drive-thru, Della knew. She sat up straight in the back seat, looking out the open window and drooling. And anxiously waited for the cylinder to drop down in the transparent pipe. The elderly teller commented on how pretty and well-behaved Della was so she dropped TWO biscuits in the cylinder. That made Della real happy and she's at daycare celebrating her reward with other dogs.

9 Likes, 2 Comments

------*Susie always kept her eye on the teller to make sure she got her tiny dog bone.*

------*She (the teller) hasn't seen the chewed Cox cable box or the legs on the bar stools....LOL!*

March 7

What? You got a bone to pick with me???

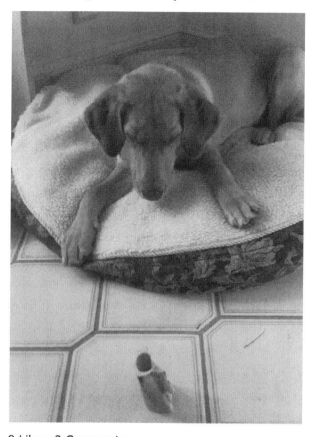

8 Likes, 2 Comments

------*Della has become a BEAUTIFUL dog!*

------*So cute....*

March 7

Had to take Della to the vet yesterday because of her recurrent loose stools that became worse in the past two days. Luckily, the vet did not find any parasites and assumed that it could be a bug Della caught from other dogs, although she still eats like an elephant. She only needs special diet for the next several days before going back to her normal food. The vet suggested white rice or cooked chicken be added to the dog food in order to "firm up her stool." So I'm really thankful for a team helper - Steve. He cooked a huge pot of rice this morning and put it in a Ziploc bag so we can scoop some out for each feeding. So far Della likes rice. Wait until we give her chicken. I guess it is now okay to give her some human food every now and then but it would be only rice and chicken!

0 Likes, 11 Comments

------*My chocolate, wrigley, has had so many health scares and has been on the rice and ground beef diet many times. Knowing her she probably plays "sick" sometimes in order to get that meal-she loves it! In all seriousness, the rice, rice and chicken, or rice and meat really works! Hope your pup feels better soon.*

------*A table spoon of canned pumpkin added to the chicken and rice will also help firm up poo. Plain, nonfat yogurt would also be a good add.*

------*Actually, giving pumpkin to dogs is a laxative and does not firm up.*

------*Maybe a food allergy? They can develop them at any age. Here's an article I wrote about our trouble with food allergies: http://dogspired.com/personal-stories/a-case-of-the-bad-poopies/*

------*We have had to put Susie on the white rice and chicken diet several times due to loose stool. It always seems to work. Now she is only given Purina ONE rice and chicken dry dog food.*

------*aw hope Della will feel better, you know feeding the dogs off from our table food aren't good for them. I know its hard not to feed them our food! Lol*

------*Actually, some "people food" is really good for a dog. Many fruits, veggies and fresh meats regularly added to their diet is quite healthy for them. Once Della is over her stomach upset, daily treats of these foods, (read up on which are best and which should be avoided), is a good idea.*

------*(From Nora the breeder) That is surprising. Sterling Meadows is one of the best kennels around. They are normally pretty clean. I suppose they can't monitor sick animals that come to their kennels. Hope Della is doing better real soon!*

------*(Bainy replies) Nora, it's still not certain whether or not Della caught a bug or even has it. It could be something else such as too much peanut butter I've been treating her. But she is doing much better today, though half of her stool is still loose but not as bad as yesterday. And she's on medication that is supposed to firm up her stool. I don't think it was Sterling Meadows - Della did love it and the staff loved her too. I would take her back there if we go away for more than 4 or 5 days. And that place has a great pasture for dogs to play around. Only for a weekend trip we would take Della to the new kennel here in Norfolk, only two miles away. So we plan to use both kennels in the long run. Besides, Della is just so lovable and a well-behaved puppy - she knows not to jump on furniture or even chew anything in the house if let loose. She is smart!*

------*ahh we have all gone that route. try getting her back to dog food - you will need some trickery!*

------*it depends on how much pumpkin, a little goes a long way.*

March 8

Della is doing better so far with digesting food. Rice has helped quite a bit. But spring is coming with toxic plants. I'm glad I was home yesterday when Della started eating nandina berries which can be fatal if eaten in a large quantity. I immediately stopped Della and cut off all those pretty red berries and threw them away. She later went back there and looked for the berries and gave up. It is scary about what pets eat in the yard. I wish a scarecrow would work with the dogs!

1 Like, 0 Comments

March 9

Something dawned on me about Della: She very rarely barks. She would only whine or howl or squeal in delight but still not often. Steve says the only time Della does bark is when she has to relieve in the middle of night. Old Mabel barks like crazy at other dogs walking by our house while Della stays mute. Why silence? Could living with a deaf owner be a factor??? C'mon, Della, I can hear with hearing aids. Bark some, please.

4 Likes, 15 Comments

------Our Lilly rarely barks! She really only barks when someone she absolutely LOOOVVVEEES is at the door. And she really just started doing that about 3 years ago. She is 10. She whines from time to time and does that Golden Retriever squeal when she is very happy.

------Brogan did not bark AT ALL his first year.....now, he barks allllll the time, especially at the dark.

------(From Gwen the caretaker at Happy Tails) She knows the sign for sit! I used it today.

------*If you miss barking I will leave my dachsies on your doorstep. They will keep you plenty entertained!!*

------*Libby barks enough for the both of them!*

------*She probably knows that she can only do so much before she crosses over the line of tolerance. Barking might do that!*

------*I also bark when I need to relieve in the middle of the night.*

------*My dog doesn't bark much either, except when she wants us to protect her from something in the middle of the night!*

------*lol same thing with my Bella who seldom barks, guess they figured out that we're deaf so why should they bother with barking? Ha*

------*does Mabel have hound in her? My Scooby barks his little face off if anyone walks by our house.*

------*I was always happy our dogs weren't marathon barkers, the neighbor's dogs were and it drove me insane. One of mine was a marathon squeaker/whiner tho when he was left alone and that got really annoying.*

------*Bainy, believe it or not, Desmond rarely barks at home. He must be "intensely" wanting a treat I'm "holding off" or desperately need to go out. Even then, it's just a woof of 'demand" or whining.*

------*I also once had a brown lab whose voice I NEVER heard in two year, mother of my black lab who only howled at night...outside like a wolf. BE thankful Della is not a 'barker"....very difficult to 'train out of them".*

------*I had a german shepherd 8 years old when Jay got a Black lab puppy. Mac was very protective and barked at all intruders, Luca (the lab) never barked at anything. The night after we had to put Mac down we heard this barking and could not figure out what it was. Then we saw Luca running the perimeter and barking just like Mac had guess she decided it was now her role.*

March 10

It's always interesting to see how a dog behaves after each meal. I usually place Della's bowl outside about 10 or 15 feet away from the side door that has a doorstep. Once Della is done eating, she picks up the empty bowl in her mouth and drops it on the doorstep and waits. She is probably asking for another meal, though she's been fed aplenty. No wonder I always come home to find an empty bowl on the doorstep. Maybe I'll try to place her dinner about 75 feet away out on the grass and see if the bowl has "crawled" back to the doorstep...

0 Likes, 6 Comments

------*dont you know a Lab is always starving*

------*That is so cute! She is really smart. "fill it up please!"*

------*yes my sis in law's dog border collie always picks her bowl when its empty...she must have food in her bowl..*

------*Oh they always gave us all kinds of excuses that they're hungry just like us humans, don't they?*

------*I'm starting to feel bad for them, but at the same time don't we human beings feel that, too?*

------*my dogs tell time...dinner time*

March 11

Why is it that yellow Labs have a thing for garden gloves? First, Olive launched for ours as soon as we put them on. Now, Della goes after Steve's gloves, even showing more fervor than she does for food. Does it matter what type of gloves they go after?

1 Like, 2 Comments

------*I think if yellow labs go for the garden gloves then the black labs are shoe crazy. Never leave your shoes out at our house or they will be gone! As soon as one lab takes one shoe the other lab sees and goes after the other shoe - so you will lose both the right shoe and the left shoe!*

------*Sperry, all of 8 weeks old, could not keep her adorable little mouth off mine today while I was pulling weeds! She kept sneezing - maybe she has allergies??? Needless to say, I didn't accomplish everything I wanted because she was just too dang cute to not stop and play with!!!*

March 12

Looks like Della has a new boyfriend at Happy Tails...

12 Likes, 5 Comments

------*Pretty Wild Girl!!! ;)*

------*What a great picture!!!!*

------*I just love watching dogs play like that:)*

------*So cute!!!!!!!*

------*And of course she has the upper hand! What else would we expect??*

March 12

Now reading "Inside of a Dog" by Alexandra Horowitz. Amazing details on how to read your dog's mind. I'm going to improve my skills around Della so I will know what is on her mischievous mind. Yes, I will act before she catapults toward the top of my head for my reading glasses.

3 Likes, 5 Comments

------*just read that myself!*

------*Does your dog really jump at your head for your glasses? I can't stop laughing.*

------*Oh really? I ought to read that book, too! Thanks for telling us ;)*

------*Hey Bainy, this book is fiction but another "dog book" that I bet you would enjoy "The Art of Racing in the Rain". I recommend it.*

------*(Bainy replies) Good to hear from you, Lynn. Been so long since I last saw you. I did read The Art of Racing in the Rain a while ago. Amazing to know how that dog perceived things around him, especially when he first detected a brain tumor from the wife of the family even before it was diagnosed - it was from the smell. No wonder there are seizure-detecting dogs these days. Just amazing...*

March 13

No, Della, fish food is not for you. Stay out of the pond and let the goldfish eat their dinner.

3 Likes, 2 Comments

------My Rocky boy jumps in our fish pond and chases them around, not nice Rocky!!

-------You could sprinkle it on her kibbles, sorta like an exotic topping.... or sprinkles:)

March 14

Perfect sunny afternoon for yardwork after work. Every time I pull a weed, Della grabs it from my hand and tears it up on the ground. Fine, take 'em. Weeds are supposed to be loathed, destroyed, and gone for good. Do your job, Della.

2 Likes, 0 Comments

March 14

Della has a favorite neighbor, Larry Burge, who helped hide her the day of my birthday party, and she is always so excited to see him. That's why we call him "Uncle Larry" and he's known to have a very distinctive voice. Tonight Della was acting weird, whining at the gate toward the street. I looked around and saw no one, half-expecting Larry to walk by with his golden retriever, but he was nowhere to be seen. However, Della knew where Larry was. He was sitting in his brought-in lawn chair at the other neighbor's house catty corner from us, about 200 feet away and out of view. But Della recognized Larry's voice from that far. So I let her run

toward him and she nearly knocked him off the chair. That tells how a dog can recognize a voice!

8 Likes, 1 Comment

------*(From Sandy the neighbor) Joy loves him, too!*

March 15

The ball is on your left, Della!
(Taken at Happy Tails)

9 Likes, 6 Comments

------*Cutie!*

------*That's quite a splash she's making! So much fun, I'm sure*

------*I sure wish we had a "happy tails" here on the ESVA (Eastern Shore of VA), my dog would LOVE IT!! Della has the best momma ever :)*

------How often do you take Della to Happy Tails?

------(Bainy replies) Lynn, she goes there no more than 3x a week, most of the time around 4 or 5 hours at a time. Sometimes only twice a week. It's because I want Della to get used to being in our fenced yard - and spending time with me. It has worked out very well - if she had been at daycare every single day, 8 hours a day, she wouldn't know me or our yard! And Della loves socializing with other dogs so Happy Tails is a perfect place for her for a few days a week!

------i think she likes to ham for the camera

March 16

Oh geez, Della just ate a half brick of Duraflame fire starter. I looked it up on the Internet and she is expected to throw it up anytime soon which should solve the problem. Nothing toxic about the fire starter but I better keep a lighter as far away as possible...

3 Likes, 12 Comments

------Did she actually swallow it??

------(Bainy replies) She chewed it into pieces but I didn't see it. There were tiny bits on her bed.

------(From Gwen the caretaker at Happy Tails) Della, why are you not sleepy after a big day at happy tails?

------(Bainy replies) Good question, Gwen. I'm surprised. Maybe because it's Friday???

------Bainy, Dex ate 4 :(.......luckily, these do not have copper in them as that becomes the problem in terms of toxicity.......

------is there anything she doesn't eat?

------*so did she? throw it up?*

------*I'm only 9 weeks in Bainy!!! I have been laughing hysterically at your Della posts but now that I have a new puppy at home, I'm starting to worry... How old is Della? Sperry is a full time job right now!!! I am actually waiting on a pee/poop while I type craving a good night's sleep!!!*

------*(Bainy comments the next morning) News Update: No, Della did not throw up and the fire starter must've passed through as Steve said it was quite a huge pile. That dog's got an iron stomach and might as well eat a log. Imagine mixing those two...*

------*ouch i remember my dog years ago went thru boxes of tissues even chew my hearing aids!! never a dull moment*

------*That's wax in the Duraflame fire starter at Della might be attracted to for its smell. I would put those up high where she can't get to it also watch out for your eyeglasses, hearing aids (earwax in ear molds) & flip flops as dogs like stinking smells of feet too.*

------*Same thing happened to me. It turned out okay! Puppies!!!*

March 17

Now resetting the birdfeeders and filling them with safflower and thistle seeds and making these feeders as squirrelproof and Dellaproof as possible. Come on back, little innocent birds. Dinner is ready.

3 Likes, 0 Comments

March 17

Della has learned how to fish in our backyard pond - by wading back and forth and trying to bite a goldfish. So far, no catch. Fish too slippery and possibly smarter than she is.

4 Likes, 3 Comments

------*My Rocky "fishes" too*

------*She just wants some sushi!*

------*Fire up the grill, she'll get one some day!*

March 18

Now that spring is coming in a few days, Della will have many exciting adventures in our yard. She already has had a few this gorgeous sunny weekend. She is dancing and hopping around, even jumping as high as five feet into the air - to chase white butterflies. Hilarious to watch.

1 Like, 1 Comment

------*Sperry likes to EAT dirt! Just plain dirt... guess I won't have to keep buying the Eukanuba puppy food!!! Haha!*

March 19

Della thinks she's high atop her throne...
(Seriously this is about the 5th or 6th picture taken at Happy Tails of the same pose and chair in a six-month span)

13 Likes, 7 Comments

------*How cute*

------*Don't her eyes show self-importance???*

-------*"I am the boss, you are my lowly servants, OBEY ME!" :)*

------*I had a big golden who used to sit in small chairs and she would sit as though she was waiting for a treat, very prim and proper. I think they want to be on the same level as the humans.*

------*I love Della .... she is so sassy!!! :)*

------*Della sounds like she could/would get along with my two. Lucy is a labradoodle and Desi is part border collie/akita. We got to get them together.*

------*Gives her a chance to survey her kingdom from on high.*

March 19

Hmph...Della just chewed off my pretty little pink tulips. Now it looks like a pitiful flowerless clump.

3 Likes, 3 Comments

------*Picture please! I can't stop laughing*

------*She was simply following directions...two lips*

------*I have not met this dog but she rocks!*

March 20

Whenever I stretch on the floor after a workout on our StairMaster at home, Della would of course interrupt my muscle extension by walking ON me, not around me. Boy, she is heavy, all of 70 pounds and still growing. And Della does something out of affection: Nibble my forearm which sometimes hurts! But it's nice to know you're loved by a dog. I prefer an arm nibble to a big sloppy lick on the face.

1 Like, 1 Comment

------*Sperry is in the "nibbling" stage - only her 9 week old teeth are like running your arms through a weedeater!!! Haha!*

March 21

How can you prevent your dog from eating so much grass which yields a quite unpleasant pile later during the walk? Della can't seem to get enough of her salad in the yard.

0 Likes, 7 Comments

------*I dunno. Maybe add some kind of supplement that has whatever nutrients are in grass (spirulina? chlorophyll?) But you might still have the unpleasantness afterwards, not sure.*

------*They say dogs eat grass when their stomachs are upset. Good luck.*

------*You might ask your vet - she may have an upset tummy or need more roughage in her diet. Grass just tastes good! Please avoid weed killers and fertilizers. Am convinced they are responsible for two of our dogs getting lymphoma. . .*

------*Yeah you want to discourage that cuz its a good way to get worms. I actually tried growing some grass in a pot inside.*

------*I also tried adding dried seaweed to their food which helps some. You could try green beans too.*

------*Glad I read your comments Stephanie, my dog is doing the same thing. I've been pulling the grass out of her mouth.*

------*I've heard they sometimes just like the taste of it, or crave some nutrient, or have an upset stomach. It's probably some of all of those. I'd grow some chives or parsley or other green grasslike herbs and add them or other vegetables to her food, see if she likes that. Emily is right, you don't want her eating treated grass.*

March 22

Came home to see Della's nose powdered with...pollen. It's only the beginning.

1 Like, 0 Comments

March 23

Della came out of daycare wringing wet from a day in the pool. She was thrashing around in my car on the way home, rubbing her face on the back seat, rolling over, and growling with legs sticking up in the air. And finally stuck her head out the window to dry. So my car was rockin' nearly the whole way and I'm sure people had a field day of watching it...

3 Likes, 3 Comments

------*Nothing like the smell of wet dog.*

-------*Della sent the message that she had a great day.*

------*(Bainy comments) A happy growl sure does sound different from a mean growl.*

March 25

Steve just took Della for a four-mile run in the neighborhood. Is he turning my dear precious puppy into a marathon dog???

8 Likes, 3 Comments

------*(From Eric, Steve's cousin) No. He's trying to help that wrecking machine burn off some of that energy.*

------*Be careful-you don't want her to get arthritis or have joint issues.*

------*(Bainy replies) It happens only once a week, especially on weekends. Most of the time it's two miles. But today was an exception because of the rain. It has worked because Della is relaxed on her bed with her bone.*

------*Awesome!*

March 25

Thanks, Della, for the new design on my sweatshirt!

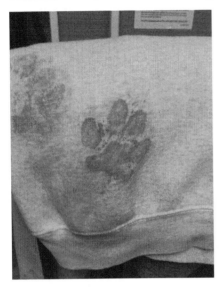

26 Likes, 8 Comments

------*Della is an artist!*

------*that's a keeper for sure!!!!*

------*I love it, you need to frame that!!!*

------*Cut it round and frame it! :)*

------*Hysterical. Good Christmas card photo!*

------*She loves her mommy!!!*

------*oh that is funny. perfect paw prints too*

------*perhaps, the cover of your book!*

March 25

From owning dogs all these years I find one thing amazing about large dogs playing with smaller dogs. When our deceased lab Olive, two years old at the time, first got Mabel as her new companion, she looked down at this four-month-old mutt and wrapped her arm around Mabel as if to say, "Hey, I'm bigger than you." That arm gesture continued for many years because Mabel remained a head shorter than Olive who did not want her own bigger size to be overlooked. Well, Della is doing exactly the same thing to poor old Mabel, almost 16 now, who has shrunk somewhat. So I will try to take a picture of Della wrapping her arm over Mabel and saying, "Hey, I'm no longer a tiny little puppy so grin and bear it."

2 Likes, 0 Comments

March 26

Came home to see old Mabel's black fur covered with a layer of pollen. Della? It's hard to tell because she is a yellow dog...

3 Likes, 1 Comment

------*Even my sunglasses had pollen on them after a short trip out, weird.*

March 26

Della, don't even think about snapping up a bee. You'll pay a huge price.

2 Likes, 1 Comment

------*Sperry seems to have a love for dried worms on the concrete!!! UGH!!!*

March 27

Since there is always something going on with Della, who turns 10 months old today, I've decided to end the book "Della on Facebook" on my birthday in July instead of her first birthday in May. So readers will be shown a full year of craziness from the time I turned 50 with an unexpected puppy. So please keep up with your comments and suggestions. I've always loved hearing your experiences with your pets!

18 Likes, 6 Comments

------*What a cute picture! You said unexpected. How did you end up with her then? I'd love to hear your story.*

------*(Bainy replies) Here's a one-line story: My husband surprised me with the seven-week-old Della at my 50th birthday party and I was shocked beyond belief but delighted with an addition to our childless family!*

------Oh what a present!!! We are also a childless family but our lab makes us whole.

------So sweet! I had hoped to have two or three kids, but I got one! So we filled up the house with two kitties and two doggies. I always feel blessed.

------So, had you talked about having another child? :-) David and I keep saying we've got enough, but God sends them to us. I swear we don't go looking for them. We've got four at the moment plus two that are supposed to be my brothers but ....(to be continued).

------(Bainy comments) Oh Reba, don't tell me you hoard cats...

March 27

Steve left a few piles of hardwood mulch in flower beds for me to spread but Della already did it by jumping right into the middle of each pile and rolling around. So I guess I don't have to do the work.

5 Likes, 3 Comments

------Close enough for me.

------That just put a huge smile on my face and made my day.

------I prefer pine straw, that way, Calvin doesn't track in the pine mulch.

March 28

I wish dogs could learn the food pyramid and not eat inedible stuff. Della had a bad night, throwing up grass, mulch, and God-knows-whats. She appeared to be lethargic this morning but is back to herself after sleeping quite a bit. And ate all of her lunch. Now that dog has to refrain from eating a yard. My house will

have to have a "mullet" yard this year: lots of flowers on the front yard to which Della has no access on her own and no flowers in the back yard in which she can run loose. Like that Bill Ray Cyrus haircut - business in the front and party in the back. Here comes our mullet yard...

9 Likes, 2 Comments

------*You crack me up!*

------*Luca (old long gone black lab) at 5lbs of bird seed once...looked like it had swallowed a small pig.*

March 28

Spent a glorious afternoon cleaning up the back yard. When I ruffled up a large bed by raking and weeding, several thick cotton balls came flying around, some ten feet apart. I thought, where the heck did those come from? Then I remembered. Della attacked a patio pillow back in the fall...

9 Likes, 3 Comments

------*lol*

------*I can't thank you enough for these posts. They make me bust out laughing everytime I read one. They truly put a smile on my face.*

------*Me too Bainy! It makes my day to read about Della's adventures...thanks for the free therapy!*

March 29

Waiting on the doorstep for her lunch. See where she brought her empty bowl in from around the corner...

14 Likes, 9 Comments

------*So sweet & trying to be hopeful that you will feed her at any minute..*

------*What kind of dog is Della, Bainy? :)*

------*(Bainy replies) Hungry yellow lab*

------*She is beautiful!!*

------*We have this big 'ol 120 lb lab mix who stomps on his metal bowl making a loud clanging noise to let us know he's hungry.*

------*Reggie carries his out to the kitchen when he wants more.*

March 30

I think I know why Della has had loose bowels until just recently. It's the type of "healthy" dog food which I won't describe here. I feel that many expensive brands have too much vitamins and minerals these days. Consider our lab Olive who lived to be almost 13 and still had a hearty appetite right up to the end of her life - eating the same brand since she was a puppy and loved it. And...Mabel is still living, almost 16, and eating that same brand too. So I plan to feed Della the same Pedigree brand and see how she does. She was recently fed Mabel's food and her stool now looks so much better, no longer runny. And Della is active enough to digest old-fashioned ingredients such as meat and fat, not only vitamins and minerals. Dogs are carnivores, right? I am going to keep an eye on Della's diet and its outcomes in the next week or so. If she has no problem with it, then we will stick with the same brand for many years to come.

0 Likes, 10 Comments

------*we tried many of the "premium" brand foods with Libby and she didnt do very good with any of them! We ended up with Purina One and she does great with that.*

------*Susie eats Purina One also and we've had very few problems.*

------*i've tried many of the TOP rated premium brands, most of them were about $60-$70 a bag..had no complaints but we finally found one we LOVE, plus it's holistic, it's called VERUS, not sure if you've tried it yet but my dog does wonderfully on it :) Good luck w/ Della, she sure is a cutie!*

------*Some of the best quality dog foods are just too rich for some dogs. However, research shows with dog food you truly get what you pay for. Since meat should be the first ingredient you might at least want to know it's a good quality meat. As for longevity, I think it is determined by genetics more than anything else.*

------*My dog loves Acana grain free...a carnivore delight.*

------*Um, Bainy? Are you seriously posting a notice on facebook about the state of your dogs turds? Not to totally bust your chops here, but come on....*

------*agree with Eric*

------*(Bainy replies) Eric, get a dog. You'll understand. Grin.*

------*I'm getting a lab puppy next month. What food do you recommend?*

------*dogs are omnivores like us, cats are carnivores*

March 30

During our walk just a few minutes ago, a mailman in his van pulled up and slid the door open and handed a biscuit to Della. I am impressed that she didn't give the mailman a bite in return.

1 Like, 0 Comments

March 31

I'm preparing myself for the loss of my other dog Mabel. It could be in a few days or a few months as she suddenly became ill this morning with nausea and loss of balance. The vet assumed a stroke or tumor but found that Mabel has a severe ear infection that usually causes disorientation as well. So her progress is unknown. In my heart I know it's old age. Sixteen years for a 45-pound mutt are a long time. Resting at home, Mabel is still wobbly and cannot look straight but wags her tail whenever she sees me. Mabel has been amazing in the past five years since her companion Olive passed away. She stopped being active and slept a lot. However, a few months after Della came along, Mabel

suddenly wanted to play with her, even running hard after the ball every morning. At first I wanted to stop such an ancient dog for fear of a heart attack but then decided that it was her bucket list. Mabel has had a lot of fun with Della. That's what I am grateful for: an old dog and a puppy at the same time.

22 Likes, 33 Comments

------*You know, Bainy, God has a way of knowing when to send a new puppy to a family. Della was your "send." It is how it works.*

------*You, Steve, Olive, and Della have given Mabel several wonderful lives! She won the lotto when she came into your family.*

------*Our furry family members wrap themselves around our hearts like no one else can! It's so hard to lose them but having a crazy puppy around will certainly help. Been there a few times. :(*

------*Yep Bainy, young friends keep us young. Mabel is teaching all of us a lesson.*

------*In ur heart she will always be. Mabel rocks! Della's keeping her young.*

March 31

Steve can no longer say, "What was I thinking?" after deciding in the last minute to get me a puppy. I thank God for Della because she is cheering me up while I am sad about Mabel's worsening condition. I may have to take her to emergency vet tomorrow morning if she still cannot stand up or drink water. Anyway, Della is now bugging me to play with her long-lost favorite Kong ball she just found behind the grate after two months. Dogs do have their particular favorite balls and I wonder if it has to do with the smell?

1 Like, 7 Comments

------*When a door closes...a window opens.*

------*So sorry to hear about Mabel. Della may be trying to take your mind off the sadness. They can sense when something is wrong. ;-(*

------*That's why I got Bella when Princess turned ten. And they loved this Kong ball that they'd have a tug war with it all the time so I just got them an extra ball, and still Bella wanted them both to herself.*

April 1

A little old lady strolling in the neighborhood and chatting with me was indeed a lucky person because she did not get jumped on by Della who has learned a few things about age difference. Once that lady walked away, Della suddenly jumped up and stamped her huge paws on my shoulders. I should be flattered that she knows I'm younger but still a dog owner. Dogs know the difference between little old ladies and dog owners, don't they?

8 Likes, 1 Comment

------*(From the elderly neighbor) Now I can walk by your house and not worry about Della!*

April 3

Mabel is not doing better and it may not be only the middle ear infection. It can be a combination of age-related problems. So...it'll be her time today. Yes, it's been a sad week but I'm grateful for her good long life and her last hard run with Della just four days ago. Mabel, you've been a great dog.

8 Likes, 48 Comments

(All of the comments expressed understanding and none mentioned Della)

April 3

Mabel is now in a better place. It helped to come home to an oblivious, cheerful puppy jumping on me and licking my tears.

14 Likes, 57 Comments

------She is up in doggie heaven free of suffering. So sorry. It is so sad to lose a pet. Thank goodness for your "puppy"! (she looks pretty big to me)

------She is in heaven with Freda's dog Murphy, eating as many treats as she wants. So glad you have Della to ease the painful loss.

------Oh, Bainy, I'm so sorry. You made a courageous decision for your friend. You and Steve will be in my prayers as you grieve the loss of sweet Mabel. Hold tight to Della, as she will be of great comfort to you.

------So sorry for your loss. Very glad Della is there for you.

------Oh, Bainy, I am so sorry. Dogs have a way of weaving themselves into your heart, and it is so very hard to part with them. And then you find yourself looking for them around every corner in their usual spots. I am thinking of you this week.

------:-(:-(:-(so very sorry for your loss. Dog is God spelled backwards. I'm glad Della gave you some love when you got home.

------Bless her sweet doggie heart, in doggie heaven. She has gone to meet the morning stars, as my mother used to say.

------Bainy, so sorry for your loss. Tell Della to give you some extra puppy hugs today.

------Sorry for your loss. Murphy will show her where the kibble is kept in Heaven.

------I am so sorry! Della knows how you are feeling. She will take care of you. Hugs tight!

------) ; Sad for the human heart. Mabel isn't suffering or in pain, she's romping with your other dog and safe in God's arms. My thoughts are with you all now.

------Bainy, I'm so very sorry to hear about Mabel. You have been good to her and she to you. I 'm happy that you have Della to ease some of the sorrow!

April 3

Thank you all for your kind words about my dog Mabel. She is back with her old friend Olive and howling again at the siren (she stopped when losing her hearing a few years ago). Since Olive knew Mabel could not swim far into the ocean because of her small feet, she with her huge webbed feet went out to get the ball, not afraid of big waves. Mabel always waited on the shore as she knew what Olive was going to do out of consideration. She opened her mouth for Olive to drop the ball into it. A swimmer doing a favor for a non-swimmer. Those two are having a nice splashy reunion up there.

32 Likes, 18 Comments

------The big dog condo in the sky is much happier now.

------Thinking of you...have you seen the poems/videos of the rainbow bridge...

------The thought of the two of them having fun again makes it so bittersweet...this is the hardest part about having pets. The years of fun and companionship seem to melt away with this pain...but just keep remembering how much she enjoyed being with you! We are SO lucky to have our animals!

------Bainy, this reminds me of the time - an wakeful one, when we learned our yellow lab, Blondie, was hit by a car and died. The dilemma was how

to tell Meredith who at the time was 4 years old....as we approached her very tenderly, and told her what happened we were a bit surprised when her face lit up - when she said "now Tigger (our recently deceased beloved cat) has someone to play with in heaven." out of the mouths of babes come wisdom! Pet heaven must be a very special place!

------Sorry Bainy, your furry pals were obviously not just friends by family and Mabel will surely be missed !! It is truly a loss that leaves a gap in your heart. Hopefully Della will help to heal the wound !! :)

April 4

It was bittersweet this morning waking up to only one dog but Della already rejuvenated me for the day.

4 Likes, 2 Comments

------It's amazing how the energy of another animal pulls us back out into life again....

------glad that Della keeps you going though. Xx

April 4

There she goes again...Always high and mighty on the chair at Happy Tails.

19 Likes, 5 Comments

------*Della sure has matured into a beautiful dog!*

------*Della is getting big and loves you.*

------*Gorgeous Della! :)*

------*There is poise and class going on here!!*

------*"I am the Queen"!*

April 6

A lady asked, "What's your puppy's name?"
"Della," I replied.
"Oh, Bella!"
"No," I tried to explain, "Della with a D."
The lady thought and said, "Oh, you mean Dolly..."
"No, not Dolly. Della. D-e-l-l-a. She was named after my
husband's grandmother."
"Oh, I got it. Come here, Bella..."

12 Likes, 13 Comments

------*Tell her Della like Della Reese.*

------*lady-get-a-hearing-aid...........*

------*Funny, she can't say Della...*

------*Did she have a hearing impairment? Or perhaps there was just bad wiring. :). Too funny.*

------*I have had the same problem with our golden "Misty" people keep calling her Missy.*

------*Listening is an art. . .obviously this person is no artist!*

------*Some folks go through life and never get it!!*

------*I had a similar experience with my dog Bebe - this woman really wanted her to be named PHOEBE - LOL.*

April 8

Happy Easter to everyone! Della will have her first hard-boiled
egg for breakfast. But it's not colored...

11 Likes, 2 Comments

------Libby loves eggs

------My two get a little scrambled egg now and then. They love it.

April 8

Time to order another cord of firewood

5 Likes, 3 Comments

------Happy Easter!!!

------Happy Eater Y'all!

------At least it's not your Easter bonnet

April 8

After a wonderful Easter picnic here with half of my family, Steve pulled out two chairs, placed them in the rose garden, dug a hole, and had me read a prayer by St. Francis of Assisi - before spreading Mabel's ashes into the hole. It was inches away where Olive the lab, Ernie the cat, and Norm my premarital cat were also buried in ash form. Then we reminisced about how great a dog Mabel was. Honestly, I don't think she would mind if we were celebrating her life while Steve had a beer and I had wine...

32 Likes, 10 Comments

------*Sweet!!!*

------*We should all have such a great send off! Bravo Mabel! To be so fondly remembered is a wonderful gift!*

------*Well done!*

April 9

I cannot find a fish net anywhere in this entire city of Norfolk. Not even Bob's Gun and Tackle carries one. I guess I will drive several miles to Lowe's or Home Depot. How can I scoop out toxic camellia petals and one dead fish from the fishpond? Della, YOU scoop them out because you destroyed our good fish net and even bent it in half.

1 Like, 13 Comments

(All of these comments tell where I can buy one!)

April 10

Nothing new about Della today but she's still one crazy puppy...That's all I can say!

9 Likes, 4 Comments

------So sorry she hasn't done something today.... I look forward to her mischief!!

------(Bainy replies) Well, just a minor mischief this evening...Della grabbed a half-full water bottle off the kitchen table and soaked her bed by chewing it!

------Glad to hear she is adjusting to Mabel's absence! Bless her heart!

------our four 9-week-old pups are crazy and playful with their momma.

April 12

It's been two weeks since we switched Della's diet from a fancy brand to a grocery-store brand and she has been much more energetic with more firmed-up stool (Sorry, my dear brother Harvey, just the LAST doo doo dispatch, I promise). So that means Della has meat on her bones, not only minerals and vitamins you find 100% in a fancy brand. I am certain Della will lead a voracious, healthy life with the same brand we had fed to our previous dogs who lived past their longevities. Besides, that brand is not made in China so we're all safe!

4 Likes, 5 Comments

------(Bainy's brother Harvey comments) it's never too late for a Della stool update

------Awe Poo! I look forward to the latest doo doo! At least it's not the same s**t that's in the media!

------What brand did you switch to? My dogs have been eating Iams for years. The little processing machines produce firm, non stinky poo suitable for mounting!

------non stinky?!?!?! Not mine, and they are on Iams! Yeesh, I hate poo!

------You cant really tell where it comes from cuz they only have to list if they buy directly from China.

April 12

Reader's Digest now has an interesting article: "50 Secrets Your Vet Won't Tell You." I found one quite funny; a medical director of an Illinois vet hospital quotes, "People always ask, 'How do you handle pit bulls, Rottweilers, and German shepherds?' The truth is, the dogs that scare me most are the little Chihuahuas. They're much more likely to bite." I'm relieved to have a nice, humble Lab!

6 Likes, 5 Comments

------in my opinion Chihuahuas are way more dangerous then pitbulls. They go right for the ankles & if someone is holding them they go for your jugular...we know from experience! Thank the lord for Labs ♥

-------LOL There are SO many Chihuahuas in CA; you see them everywhere even out running with their people. It seems people tend to think that since these dogs are so small they really don't need much training, but without it they often become little devils.

------Gotta agree, my German Shepherd is all bark!!

------So it's "Short Dog Syndrome"...

------My sister called her lab "body of steel, head of mush" and I thought it was hilarious!

April 12

We made a mistake of installing a folding door to our pantry during the 1998 house renovation. Della has found a trick of pushing one end of the door to the left with her snout and folding it open to access dog food. A new solid door with a doorknob will be considered over the weekend.

3 Likes, 10 Comments

------*What about putting the dog food in a large plastic tub with a lid.*

------*(Bainy replies) We did. But Della still tries to get into the pantry no matter what.*

------*Della is such a smart girl. Be sure you get a doorknob she can't figure out!*

------*We got a clear sliding clip that locks the door flat in place, to keep it from folding open... You just slide it aside when you want to open it. It fits over the top of the door :)*

------*You sure Della hasn't put in for an opposible thumb transplant?*

------*Smart as a whip!*

------*Please do not keep the dog food in the bag if she can get to it. A friend's beloved dog got in to theirs - they came home & found the dog suffocated with his head in the bag. It was so sad for their family (and it was a large, strong dog).*

------*(Bainy replies) Jenny, we pour dog food into the bin right away and discard the bag. I know bags are tricky. So sorry about your friend's dog.*

------*What a smarty dog, Della! Bainy, you will need to "childproof" the door to prevent her going into the pantry to retrieve the dog food.*

------*We had that problem, too. A simple hook and eye latch placed up high took care of it.*

April 13

Della will have to take serious swimming lessons as I just learned from Happy Tails that she would get into the pool but does not know how to swim. Despite her huge webbed feet, Della lets her hind legs drag while using her front ones to paddle fiercely. I wonder if there is anything such as dog flippers that would help her kick from behind???

3 Likes, 4 Comments

------*it will come to her!*

------*Dud. Hence the term doggie paddle!#?*

------*She would look really cute with an innertube...*

------*Maybe they should tie her front paws together, swim or sink! ;-)*

April 14

Doing one household chore on a Saturday morning, once every two or three weeks: Vacuum Della's three-foot-wide round bed, unzip and yank the cover out, throw it into the washer with a large dose of Tide, fluff up the bed cushion by six inches thicker, mop the kitchen floor, transfer the clean cover to the dryer, wait, and finally push the thickened bed cushion inside the cover, zip it up, and call Della over.

4 Likes, 3 Comments

------*Bainy, any more hints? I'm picking up my lab pup and bringing him home on Friday. I bought food, food and water bowls, treats, something to chew on for the 7 hour ride home, and a new collar and leash. Any other suggestions are welcomed and appreciated! I am going to crate and have been reading Water dog.*

------*How lucky can Della get!*

------*(Bainy replies) Mary, I cannot wait to meet your unusual silver Lab pup. Please call or email me so we can make plans for you and pup to come by here to play with Della. I also talked to Nancy and urged her to get the other pup. That's what we in our 50's need!*

April 15

Della, can't you let me enjoy my coffee and Sunday paper out on the patio? I'll play ball with you in a minute...

3 Likes, 1 Comment

------*yeah .. I let puppies out of big crate ... They play for a while before they go nap...*

April 16

After Happy Tails...preferring cool floor over her fluffy bed on a hot day.

13 Likes, 2 Comments

------Don't we all?

------a tired lab is a good dog

April 17

A morning greeting from your dog can certainly wake you up even before coffee. Here's Della suddenly wagging her tail, dancing through my legs back and forth, then sticking her head up between my upper legs, and urging me to bend over to give her a chest rub. In return I get licks on my ears. A good way to jump start my day!

9 Likes, 3 Comments

------Dogs do that for you! Love you no matter what!

------As soon as either of us even mildly stir first thing in the morning, our Bertie girl likes to jump in between us and snuggle. She likes to bring us her toy duck, Mallard J. Filmore, or more affectionately known as Duckie!!!!

------So cute!!!!!!!!!!!

April 17

Oh swell...Della caught a three-inch-long goldfish and was about to eat it when I caught her. Her snout seems to work better than a fishing rod...

0 Likes, 3 Comments

------jake left a dead rat in the middle of the living room floor. Not sure if it concerns me more that he found it or that he killed it

------Another Della post to make my day!

------*I guess you weren't able to find that pond net you were talking about getting. Did she get it from your pond? Silly girl*

April 18

Someone asked me today if Della sleeps on our bed. Our human bed upstairs??? The answer is no, absolutely not. It'd be like sleeping with a Mexican jumping bean as dogs have been known to change sleeping positions every ten minutes. Della has her very own bed downstairs in the kitchen as well as a smaller one in her open grate where she can switch to anytime she wants. She's got two beds and we have only one. We're all content.

3 Likes, 2 Comments

------*I bet she would curl up into the smallest ball and never move all night.*

------*Sallie sleeps on my bed but only in the winter or when it is cold cuz she is a good heater :) its tough getting her out of the habit due to summer and soon ill e off to college so i dont want her to miss me too much when im gone*

April 19

Big entertainment here this morning: Della was fiercely attacking a laser beam emitting from Steve's pen, chasing the red dot all over the room and on the walls. Will have to take a video the next time.

2 Likes, 2 Comments

------*Never a dull moment with Della around!*

------*Libby loves the lazer pen too!*

April 19

"New Meaning to Ninja!"
(Quoted by Jana of Happy Tails - thanks for making your place FUN for Della!)

6 Likes, 3 Comments

------*Omg your Della looked more wild than my Bella! Are you sure she s not a guy, but a gal? ;)*

------*I see Desmond looking on wondering when it would be his turn!*

------*Amazing! If I could twist and jump like that I could make lots of money! LOL*

April 19

Hot Diggity Dog! Just counted Facebook posts on Della starting on my birthday last July up to now. And three more months before the end of "Della on Facebook" which will show one full year of puppyhood regenerating enough for a 50-year-old woman. So far, the post count is 268. Many more to come - if you don't get tired of it!

3 Likes, 8 Comments

------*You should get a FB page for her!!*

------*I'm not surprised as you sure LOVE to talk about that young rambunctious blondie pup you got! ;) So am I in love with my lil crazy Golden pup Bella, too.*

------*Never got tired of reading your comments about Della almost daily :) xx*

------*She need her own facebook page my friend's cat has one*

------*Keep them coming! Reading your posts is FUN!*

------*I think you need to continue until lab puppyhood is over. At about age four!*

------*4, Barbara? No Way!*

April 21

Della is hardly moving this morning because she had a new buddy over last night that outran her back and forth in the yard. "Lily", recently adopted by the Swartz family, is a 10-month-old black Lab/Whippet mix. Della and Lily played so hard that they constantly jumped into two of our fishponds to cool off. Good to wear them out before a rainy weekend!

3 Likes, 4 Comments

------*That should buy you a few hours. LOL!*

------*Let me know when della needs a new playmate. Sophie's ready!!!*

------*(Bainy replies) Come on over anytime today. We'll be here!*

------*I just met Lily this morning:)*

April 21

Jumping into the fishpond 25 times in the past two days does not make you any cleaner. Della smells like a fish shack. So she is bound for a heavy scrub with dog shampoo. I think a garden hose would work better than a bathtub...

1 Like, 6 Comments

------*Good luck!!!!!!! Someone needs to invent a TINY car wash for dogs.*

------*I think a trip through the carwash might do it:)*

------*You should see how Elle smells after a romp in the mud.*

------*perhaps you should consider giving up the goldfish pond and close it or if you'd mind keeping giving her frequent baths then it's up to you! ;)*

------*Reminds me of a cartoon where a male dog is smitten by a female dog and says, "Sophie, I don't know what you rolled in, but it's divine!"*

------*That wouldn't be any fun.*

April 21

Della eats ice cubes like candy. No problem. No calories.

7 Likes, 4 Comments

------*Della may be so hungry soon! Watch out! Ha*

------*So does Elle. Ice is fun.*

------*Sperry runs to the kitchen every time I'm getting ice!!! I think Kevin wants to teach her to chill a beer & then bring it to him!!! 12 weeks old & she's already retrieving the newspaper every morning!!! Fetching a cold beer??? Doable! Ha! Now... If I can get her to make a martini & stop peeing in the house, she'd be the perfect dog!!! :-)*

------*our dogs LOVE ice cubes also. It's loud when they start crunching.*

April 22

Taking up the whole office on a rainy Sunday...

14 Likes, 4 Comments

------*She does have some long legs!*

------*She looks like a dang gazelle!*

------*Peaceful!*

------*It's all about the dog :)*

April 23

I'm glad Della is open to options. She is a yard dog on pretty, warm days. And she is a daycare dog on rainy days and whenever she wants to party. This morning Della looked out the window at the imminent rain and whined. It's because she wanted to socialize. So off to Happy Tails.

6 Likes, 3 Comments

------Desmond is on 'rest" duty as he and Della were wrestling so much he pulled a shoulder 'something"! They play rough!

------(Bainy replies) I'm so sorry it was Della pulling your dog's shoulder...

------You're a good mom!

April 23

Just heard Della had caused a stampede at the daycare. She appears to be the only one that knows how to unlock the gate by pushing up the lever above her head. Well, Della managed to let 30 dogs out of the large pen into the hall. The whole place ran amok. I swear I did NOT teach her that...

15 Likes, 16 Comments

------LOL!

------Way cool! Wish I'd been there with a camera! Breakout!

------Love it! Smart doggy

------Wow, another smart trick on Della's part.

------Your book is going to be a best-seller...you can't make this stuff up!!!

------*(From Jana the owner of Happy Tails) Bainy, Bainy, Bainy..... oh Della, Della, Della..... girlfriend let them all out THREE TIMES! I kept scolding my staff to shut the gate. When I finally saw what was happening I couldn't stop laughing. If there is trouble to be found, my sweet Della will find it.*

------*Della is one smart puppy!*

------*(Bainy comments) I'm gonna ask Nora the breeder where Della got that trick. It was NOT me. Hey Nora???*

------*I had a dog that would do that to every door he found. and I never taught him either.*

------*My Desi knows how to push the sliding door open. He's a gentleman and opens it for Lucy to go through first. How about that? Dogs are smarter than you think.*

------*(Nora the breeder replies to Bainy) Sure you didn't! I have a horse who opened her stall door, and proceeded to open all the stall doors to let her friends eat the alfalfa hay someone had left in the hallway of the barn. Good thing they all didn't get sick.*

------*Problem child/dog..LMAO*

------*gifted child*

------*Lol are you sure that she's not related to Marley? :)*

April 23

(Bainy Cyrus to Happy Tails)

Hey Jana, is it really true that Della released 30 dogs from the pen???

1 Like, 3 Comments

------*(Jana replies) YEP!!!! Laughing so hard. If she teaches the other dogs her super human tricks, I am in serious trouble. She is so smart and is so naughty! I love it!*

------*(Bainy comments) Honest to God, I have no idea where she got the trick...I'm gonna ask Nora the breeder. Nora?*

------*(From Jesse the Happy Tails caretaker) Who let the dogs out , woof woof woof woof DELLA let the dogs out woof woof woof woof woof ! :-)*

April 24

Considering what happened at the daycare yesterday, I better keep Della away from penitentiaries...

1 Like, 2 Comments

------*Lol bet the daycare people will keep Della in bay from now on!*

------*She will certainly get their respect and attention!*

April 27

I don't believe it...Della managed to crawl over the three-foot-tall lattice fence and reach the top of the hot tub cover and grab our new fishing net right off the cover and chew a hole in it. Number Two Gone. What's about fishing nets she is so attracted to???

1 Like, 1 Comment

------*Smells good!*

April 28

We don't give Della table scraps as her diet consists of strictly dog food and biscuits but occasional peanut butter and steak bits. Yes, she goes crazy over all of these foods but last night she went into a maniacal frenzy over her first spoonful of ice cream. Her eyes bulged like Marty Feldman's and she would not stop licking the empty spoon. And even tried to eat it. Della, wait until your first birthday in late May when you get a bowlful of peanut butter ice cream. It'll be one hell of a party...

8 Likes, 2 Comments

------What brand do u feed Della?

------(Bainy replies) Pedigree - safe and made in America!

April 29

When Della was a tiny little thing last summer, she quickly learned the trick of stealing Steve's homegrown tomatoes by sneaking under the fishnet held down by bricks. Not this year. Steve just installed a temporary chain link fence around his newly planted tomato plants. Hopefully, that will keep a nearly full-grown lab from tomato theft. I guarantee Della won't be able to get over or under so we're destined for our delicious BLTs.

1 Like, 3 Comments

------Good luck...my sister-in-law's dog climbs chain fences :P

------We thought that about our dog, Boomer, years ago. . .he climbed up and over the fence. . .

------(Bainy comments) Oh c'mon, guys, don't burst my bubble.

April 30

New Nylabone for Della. Indestructible, undestroyable, imperishable, indissoluble, INVINCIBLE.
Do you want to bet???

5 Likes, 15 Comments

------*I give it about 10 minutes...*

------*I bought a similar Nylabone for Mac on Friday. In one hour, he chewed the whole end off, and then of course, got sick...*

------*these are what I have for Libby. Have lasted about 6 months now!*

------*Would that make it "inDELLAble"?*

------*My dogs haven't destroyed those yet, and one eats bricks and beer cans. However, when they leave them in the middle of the floor and I step on them they hurt like s..t!*

------*Yes Karen!! I HATE when I step on Libby's Nylabone!*

------*let us know the outcome*

------*If they were really indestructible there would be a money-back guarantee! 90 minutes, tops.*

------That's scary looking! But whatever it takes. Let me know how it works. I'm sure I'll need one for Sofie!

------Bainy, the only bone I swear by for our voracious chewers is the Nylabone Dura Chew... And they do have a warranty if you're not satisfied :) best bone ever. ! :)

------Careful, Brogan had the same one and got the white tips off in nothing flat, which then become an extreme choking hazard.....

------Ann, agreed!

------Our Layla had hers destroyed in a day!

------Our weimaraner can destroy that within an hour. The only toy she doesn't destroy is "kong" and only the black ones.

April 30

Pinned down by a Bassethound at Happy Tails...

9 Likes, 3 Comments

------Looks like pure joy!

------*Bassets are basically big dogs with short legs, so I can see that happening .... At least for a brief moment.*

------*As someone who's had basset hounds my entire life (including my current love who looks an awful lot like this big fella), they are hugely playful and love to "spar" with a friend; cutest thing looking at this picture!*

May 2, 2012

Della has a new toy in the back yard: FROGS!!!

6 Likes, 6 Comments

------*Good eatin'*

------*Plastic or real? Eh heh*

------*If you go to the deep south, don't let her eat buffo toads (sp?) They are highly poisonous.*

------*So now Steve won't have to relocate them???*

(To explain the last question, in the past few seasons I've been posting about Steve collecting and relocating frogs to a pond across the city because they keep him awake at night.

------*(Bainy replies) He still has to, Carolyn. Too much noise for him at night!*

------*I understand. We had a couple a long time ago in Norfolk, that we used to travel to Aspen with before we moved there. Frogs got to be a joke and we had a "frog" party at our house on Fairfax Ave for them. Everyone brought frogs of some kind or description-pictures, etc...except one person brought real frogs and put them in out fish pond...from that day forward all we heard were frogs- mostly at night...then when we moved to Mathews our "across the creek" neighbor built a fish pond for his Koi and there were weeks that all we heard were frogs. They do get to be too loud!!!*

May 3

On her usual outdoors bed, using liriope as a pillow. Life is really rough...

25 Likes, 6 Comments

------*That's cute Bainy!*

------*awww she is cute and sweet.*

------*Adorable! Liriope as a pillow? it works! ;)*

------*Awww ♥*

------*I see she has a stash of pinecones!*

------*What a little lambchop.*

May 4

Looking forward to putting Della in the Chesapeake Bay for the first time this weekend. I hope she'll finally learn to kick her back legs and stay afloat!

9 Likes, 2 Comments

------Taffy never learned to swim 'til I got in the Ocean and she swam out to rescue me!!!

------Mine gets in the pool and he has enough fat on him to float without having to kick his back feet hardly at all.

May 4

Enjoying the scenery on the Chesapeake Bay Bridge-Tunnel after being given a huge biscuit by the gate lady...

29 Likes, 1 Comment

------OMG, even the gate lady is prepared to pamper our Tidewater Pups!

May 4

Yea, Della, you're in the bay! Come on kick your back legs. If you swim, you need to do it horizontally, not vertically! You can do it!

6 Likes, 1 Comment

------Go Della....swim like a champ!!!

May 5 (Spending a weekend on the Eastern Shore)

It's 8:00 AM and Della is already in the Chesapeake Bay going after her new orange tube toy, the kind you throw for a hunting dog. And her swimming skills have improved dramatically overnight as you can now see her entire back on the water surface, not only her head and flapping front paws. Della has become an Olympic swimmer!

14 Likes, 1 Comment

------Dock Dogs next!!!!

May 5

Della has learned to swim but needs to learn not to drink the Chesapeake Bay. She will have to learn the same with the Atlantic Ocean in a few weeks.

3 Likes, 2 Comments

------one step at a time,,,,

------Think Della will notice a difference in the taste between the two? ;-)

May 5

You've heard of the King of the Hill. Now look at the Queen of the Table.

5 Likes, 1 Comment

------Precious!

May 5

Table taken. Already reserved.

18 Likes, 0 Comments

May 5

Once you treat your dog with table scraps, it's too late. Then your dog will start bugging you at the table for the rest of his/her life. Steve and I saved filet mignon bits for Della while eating dinner in our RV last night. She was only a few feet away sleeping on a rug, not even begging. It was because she did not know what a table scrap was. But she did enjoy the filet mignon right from her dog bowl mixed with a few kibbles. It's better to ALWAYS feed from a dog bowl, not a table.

9 Likes, 4 Comments

------*Now she tells me! haha (my dog is 15 years old)*

------*oh yes thats true, that's why I kept telling my family not to give them nibbles from the table scraps or else they'd keep begging!*

------*Agreed!*

------*Definitely true but they are our babies!!!!!*

May 6

Della has become a good RVing dog but I'm sure she would've made an excellent camping one, too. Either way she swims and hikes well. This past weekend she always returned to shore with the orange toy in her mouth and walked miles of nature trails here at Kiptopike State Park. And Della knows what a picnic table is for. Not only eating but also napping off the ground!

7 Likes, 2 Comments

------*Smart dog. Why put up with ants, worms, ticks, and itchy grass, if you don't have to.*

------*. . . and remind me to always use a tablecloth ;-)*

May 7

Soon to head home from an adventurous weekend on the Eastern Shore with Della. Took her for a loose walk on the beach and she chased all kinds of birds. She learned a few things about the cormorant, the kind of bird that dives underwater. As Della swam vigorously toward a cormorant, that bird had the sense to suddenly disappear under the surface. Imagine Della looking around in total perplexity and swimming in circles and wondering where the cormorant went...

3 Likes, 0 Comments

May 7

Gate Ladies on the Chesapeake Bay Bridge-Tunnel Greeting Della:

The young one on the Virginia Beach side three days ago: "Hey there! Nice-looking dog. Would you like a biscuit?" She handed Della a big store-bought biscuit the shape of a dog bone.

The older one on the Eastern Shore side this afternoon: "Well, hellooo darling!!! How ARE you doing today? Would you like a treat? It's homemade peanut butter. Here it is!!!" She handed Della a big flat biscuit the shape of a seagull.

So...take your dog for a joy ride on the Bay Bridge!

13 Likes, 2 Comments

------*what a great way to share some love!*

------*That would be a d*** expensive joy ride for our dogs. <chuckle> (The bridge-tunnel fee is $12 each way)*

May 8

Being 50 is not easy for my hormones that have gone out of whack, causing sleeplessness and occasional neuroticism. But owning a puppy has helped quite a bit. I must thank Della for taming me in many ways and she seems to work better than hormonal replacement therapy.

13 Likes, 2 Comments

------*In hindsight, a short course of HRT would have made a huge difference for me! Get yourself a bottle of black cohosh in the mean time! (And give some to Della!--only kidding.)*

------*My Tiger has helped me through it all too, Bainy.*

May 8

Dogs are sometimes eccentric. Della just stuck her head right into the chiminea, pulled out a charred firewood, carried it to her favorite spot, and started chewing it. Not even minding ashes on her nose. Should I call a behavior specialist?

5 Likes, 2 Comments

------*OMG... i will have to ponder that one!*

------*lol she must be restless and bored! :)*

May 9

Gosh, it's been a long soggy wet-dog-smell day. I need my house to smell like my own cooking.

2 Likes, 2 Comments

------*These are hard days when you have a dog!*

------*I was thinking the same thing! 2 dogs are great.... until it rains!! :)*

May 10

Because of recent rain, frogs have emerged everywhere so Della is going to have a field day with this in the next few days. However, frogs seem to be smarter than she is. Those creatures know how to immobilize themselves into dead-as-a-doorknob stones whenever threatened by a dog. During our walk Della on her leash suddenly flew ahead of me, nearly causing me to land flat on my face. She had seen a frog hopping across the street and chased it to the curb. But the frog had become a stone and refused to budge while Della tried to poke it back into action. Of course, my poor dog was befuddled while the frog did its trick. More entertaining shows to watch...

1 Like, 4 Comments

------*While we were cleaning Happy Tails last night, there was a little baby frog sitting by the chair. I should of saved it for Della!*

------*You write the best posts!*

------*Every once in a while Daisy and Riddick actually "get" the frog and they REALLY regret it because it sprays them with something horrible. they end up eating grass and shaking their heads to get the bad taste off.*

------*I had a frog in the yard that did the same thing when Tiger came around. He smelled it, touched it with his paws, nothing happened. He looked up at me and said-WTF mom?*

May 11

The Virginian Pilot just announced that dogs have the capacity to empathize with humans by yawning when they hear the sound of our yawning. So it can be contagious. I am going to test this with Della. It'd be nice if she empathizes with me when I come home dead on my feet after a long day's work.

3 Likes, 1 Comment

------*Hahahaha :)*

May 11

Della and her best neighborhood buddy Lily are out there wrestling in my yard. Chasing each other like mad. Diving into the fish pond and splashing each other. Being part Whippet, Lily can outrun and disappear into bushes before scaring Della. And Della, being the devil, can grab Lily's pink dotted collar with her teeth and shake Lily like a raggedy doll. Come on over and watch this Tom and Jerry cartoon...

7 Likes, 2 Comments

------*what kind of dog is Lily?*

------*(Bainy replies) Lab/Whippet mix*

May 12

Resting in front of the fire...

11 Likes, 4 Comments

------*How relaxing!*

------*She's had a hard day!*

------*That's cute!*

------*Looks like Della is calming down... sometimes?*

May 13

Happy Mother's Day to all the real moms - and dog moms. Della just greeted me with a lick on my ear and I feel honored!

5 Likes, 0 Comments

May 13

Welcome back to the Cyrus yard, hummingbirds. Good to see you again. Yes, there is a new dog but she can't get up to your feeders so enjoy your nice cocktail of nectarini.

5 Likes, 2 Comments

------*How are the frogs? We're thinking about putting in a waterfall & shallow steam but forgoing the pond w/ fish. No need to set out a buffet for the cat & puppy! Haha! I have seen pond less waterfalls done on HGTV.*

------*(Bainy replies) The frogs are anxiously awaiting their relocation to the ODU pond - to get away from some new beast in the yard.*

May 13

Here's wonderful news: Della ate the entire can of goldfish flakes I stupidly left on the patio table. That brand-new can was bigger than a Tall Boy. The Internet says fish food should not harm dogs but may cause an upset stomach or extensive pooping. At least Della did not eat my fish from the pond...

7 Likes, 3 Comments

------*lol...hope you ALL get through this....*

------*Thanks Bainy for sharing. We have a fish pond too so I will watch the food! We were leaving OBX yesterday so Sophie got in the car while I finished loading and thought she was being so sweet quietly waiting for me....and then I found an empty bag of pill pockets she had fished out!!*

------Fish food is popular with our dogs, too.

May 14

Della is just fine after eating the whole can of fish food. I assume she's got an iron stomach but she will have to adhere to dog food.

3 Likes, 0 Comments

May 14

OMG, Della has become a Harry Potter dog. She just walked through the wall...
(At Happy Tails)

7 Likes, 1 Comment

------Della sure looks like a happy puppy just like our Bella, too. :) ♥

May 14

I really love my job visiting my employed clients all over - in retail stores, restaurants, hotels, schools, nursing homes, and so on. But the only problem is spending a good amount of each day in my nice little Honda SUV that smells like a dog.

8 Likes, 2 Comments

------Use febreeze for pets to take out the odor in your SUV. It works. Try it.

------I'm going to get febreeze tomorrow!!

May 14

At Happy Tails: "What do you mean it's RAINING?"

22 Likes, 7 Comments

------*What a great picture!*

------*"Oh, hell no. I do not look good in stripes!"*

------*"Crazy people and their boots!"*

------*DON'T NEED ANY BOOTS! I HAVE WEB FEET!"*

May 16

Looks like the rain is over by now and the sun is back for the next several days, drying up the dirt. Della is turning yellow again.

2 Likes, 2 Comments

------*You sent it to Chesapeake!!! And it's angry cause the sky is rumbling!!!!*

------*(Bainy replies) Don't blame it on Norfolk. Chesapeake is full of farms that need irrigation.*

May 16

Dry food doesn't make a dog bowl dirty, much less leave any crumbs, but Della picks up her empty one after each meal, carries it in her mouth a few feet away, lies down, sets this stainless steel bowl between her front legs, and licks it all the way around, although there is not one bit of kibble in the bowl. She just keeps on doing it until the bowl becomes sparkling clean as liquid mercury. No need to wash it. Dry food certainly saves time.

5 Likes, 1 Comment

------*The Vita-Mix we add to Sperry's morning meal forms a crust (think egg yolks that didn't get rinsed off I'm time) in her bowl!!!! I am constantly giving it a hot water soak similar to the ones I give my broiling pan!*

May 17

My neighbor Jean, who has brought her dog Lily over to play with Della almost daily, encouraged me to go to the Meadowbrook dog park this afternoon. First there were two other neighbors with their dogs. Then almost at the same time more people and their dogs came. Good Gracious, it was one big party with 20 dogs running around and those dogs circled around Della as if to say "So, who are you? Never seen you before." Jean explained that many neighbors come to this park around 4 PM everyday so their dogs can party. So I will have to start bringing Della there, although she still has to get used to strange dogs, not like those at Happy Tails. I am glad God invented dog parks.

10 Likes, 2 Comments

------yeah same with my daughter. brings her dog to the park. dog loves the park

------Last night was "Bark in the Park" at the Diamond in Richmond. Chris' dog came back exhausted.....even though our ball team (The Flying Squirrels) lost.

May 17

Oh Lord, I've got one big kid and one big dog chasing each other while I fuss about breakable things in the house. They're now wrestling on the dining room floor. So who's that kid? My husband.

16 Likes, 1 Comment

------Oh boy!!!

May 18

First she got the red crab. Next, the moose and the bear. Now this elephant. All stolen off the shelf in the guest room. It'd nice if all these stuffed animals turned into REAL ones!

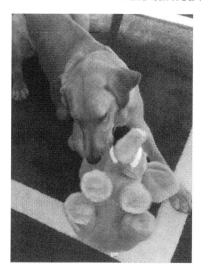

3 Likes, 1 Comment

------Stuffed animals are the only thing Meagan plays with....but she "mothers" them instead of destroying them. She has her own basket of private animals picked up at yard sales.

May 19

As a little fur ball, Della was terrified of lawn mowers and ran into bushes whenever Steve revved up his mower. Not anymore. She thinks it's time to play ball every time the mower emerges from the shed and propels toward the yard. Now Steve cannot cut the grass without interruption because Della cuts between him and

the mower - with a ball in her mouth. Maybe we will need a mower louder than a Harley to scare her off?

2 Likes, 0 Comments

May 19

Dellaproof Tomato Garden

15 Likes, 3 Comments

------*Give me some fresh tomatoes ummmm ha*

------*Or Deerproof!*

------*I used those same posts in my dog-proof garden. Got them at Lowe's, right?*

May 20

I've got only one garden glove and can't find the other one. I know who has it...

3 Likes, 4 Comments

------It will show up in 12 to 24 hours.

------Bella chewed up my favorite old garden green jean hat :(I've had it for a decade!

------I love your Della updates.

------keep digging - you will find it!

May 20

Just bought Della a new dog tag after her old metal one got rubbed and scratched so much during roughplay that her name disappeared. Petsmart has a machine in which you can laser the dog tag with the name and phone number. It was cool watching Della's name slowly form under the laser beam. And that new tag is supposed to last a long time in grass, mud, sand, pool, ocean, bay, and wherever Della gets herself dirty!

3 Likes, 1 Comment

------Yeah same thing at Petco. My daughter bought two tags for her dogs ... we watched ....

May 21

Is she yawning or laughing???
(At Happy Tails)

11 Likes, 5 Comments

------*I think she swallowed a bug!*

------*Both :)*

------*Both.*

------*Great pic!*

------*ha ha! love it!!!*

May 21

Something worries me about Della: She has a sudden big lump under the skin below her umbilical cord. I wonder if it's a bruise from playing hard. The vet said the next available time she can see Della is late tomorrow afternoon. The lump seems firm to the touch and it was not there a few days ago when I rubbed her belly. And it is close to where I found a big tick and removed it last week. Any ideas?

0 Likes, 13 Comments

------*Hernia?*

------*Sounds like an umbilical hernia. My parents' dog has one. If that's what it is, at least in Happy's case, it's not serious. She didn't need any treatment at all for hers.*

------*Is she acting okay? I was dog sitting this weekend and one of the dogs was bitten by a snake and spent the night in the pet ER. He's okay but that's what if felt like to me. It was on his cheek. Check for puncture wounds. Don't want you to have the huge bill my cousin's sister has.*

------*fatty tissue tumor? they are very common in labs*

------*Hernia?*

------*WTW! Wait to worry. She is young, healthy and is most likely nothing to drive yourself nuts over. :-)*

------*Hernia was my first thought when you said around her umbilicus. Tick bite might be infected also???? Don't worry the vet will assure you tomorrow.*

------*Hi Bainy. Our labs over the years have all had fatty tumors that are nothing to worry about. It seems to be a lab thing. I am sure your vet will have the answer!*

------*Hernia, Willa had one. Hers healed on its own when she was very young, but Della should be checked by your vet.*

------*Bainy, labs do have those fatty lipomas but she is really too young to have those quite yet. They are also fairly soft to the touch. If it is near her umbilical area, I, too wonder about a small hernia.*

------*Yes, the fatty tumors (lipomas) tend to form at a later age, and you can wrap your fingers around them, they are kind of loose under the skin, like an egg and can get quite large. Tickbite or similar might be warm and maybe a little red. I'm betting on the hernia, tho I've never had a dog with one.*

------*Let us know.*

------*How is Della?*

May 21

Thanks for your suggestions on Della's lump in her belly. I assume it's hernia since the lump appeared out of the blue. It's still big but has not affected Della's energy or appetite. She was happy to see us after we just got home from the Tides game. Della even jumped on the fence to greet us so she's obviously not in pain. But to be safe, I'll take her to the vet tomorrow. And I'm really curious as to how much Della weighs now. Almost three months ago it was 67 pounds. So I bet it's now 80 or 85.

1 Like, 2 Comments

------*Sallie has a lump on her chest. The vet says its just a fat lump. Nothing awful :)*

------*My dogs have had lumps that turned out to be those fatty ones too......but you should still have it checked out. Am praying for good news!*

May 22

Another amazing photo by Jana Underwood of Happy Tails. Taken after the one in which Della yawned. BTW, her lump has decreased in size somewhat and I am trying to keep her from being so active in the next few days. That dog was full of adrenaline the whole past weekend and yesterday, playing with Lily the neighbor and other dogs at the park and daycare!

12 Likes, 5 Comments

------*Good picture! Let us know what the vet says about her lump, hope it's not too serious and that its only minor hernia so Della ought to take it easy for awhile :)*

------*Wow! Beautiful picture.*

------*GORGEOUS!!*

------*Great picture Bainy! What a beautiful pup!*

------*(From Nora the breeder) She is so pretty Bainey. Looks like her mama, Bailey!*

May 22

The vet said Della's lump below her umbilical cord is not a hernia or fatty tissue. It is an enlarged lymph node resulting from a tick bite. So Della is on antibiotics along with delicious pill pockets. She sure hates going to a vet but can easily be lured by a biscuit or two. The good news is that Della can keep on playing. Lily and Happy Tails are still on.

12 Likes, 10 Comments

------*Glad you caught that... You're a good Momma :) Is she on Frontline Plus? Wondering if my pup is protected.*

------*Good thing you went in!*

------*Oh Happy Tailing Puppy! :) thank goodness, send xx to her for me and Bella*

------*I live in New York and ticks are horrible!! And my chocolate lab has another tick born illness and is on antibocs for 3 weeks. She has been on flea and tick medicine.*

------*Glad to hear she is ok!*

------*Go Della!*

------*Well good news that she is all right and has the right treatment:)*

------*So glad to hear all is well.*

------(Bainy replies to the first commenter) Della is not on Frontline Plus - she's on Advantage II. Seems to help so far. She got the ticks from the Eastern Shore two weekends ago.

------Thx! My pup has long fur... I need to be more vigilant :)

May 22

Thank God for the Greenies Pill Pockets - it's a great way to deceive your pet that it's a special treat but actually a HUGE antibiotic capsule. Della has no idea. With this pill pocket, she'll never spit out her medication. And those pill pockets smell like a bacon factory to dogs...

3 Likes, 5 Comments

------yeah, I went to the planet and saw the pill pockets. thats cool. I don't remember if they have those for the puppy?

------(Bainy replies) Pill pockets of the same brand come in different sizes as well as flavors. There are smaller pockets for small dogs and puppies. So look around for the pill pocket size.

------Sounds like the perfect way to get Calvin to take his monthly flea pill.

------Word of warning...the duck flavored pill pockets smell HORRIBLE! Izzy loves them but they stink up the entire house.

------(Bainy replies) Bought the chicken flavor which smells strongly also and those pill pockets are kept refrigerated so that helps...

May 23

Is it safe for Della to run like a racehorse with Lily in our yard while she is on two types of antibiotics? So far, her nymph node bitten by a tick has shrunk just a little bit but she has to take

antibiotics for two weeks. I am kinda nervous about the side effects such as vomiting and diarrhea. Isn't it a pain that every single type of medication, for both dogs and humans, has its side effects?

2 Likes, 1 Comment

------*IMO, let her play. She'd probably be more stressed if she weren't allowed to exercise. So many of the dogs I rescued had ticks and tick-borne diseases requiring antibiotics, but none suffered any immediate or long term adverse effects from the problem or the treatment.*

May 24

Della doesn't dig too much but when she does, she tries to go down about a couple feet. Her makeshift holes are usually narrow, shaping like upside down cones, not like a swimming pool. Before Della goes that far deep down, I put a brick in the hole. Then she would stop. It works. Of course, she would later dig another hole. Another brick thrown in there. Paws in surrender. I am going to order more bricks...

5 Likes, 2 Comments

------*Sperry now seems to have an affinity for my woodwork in the house!!! Help, Bainy!!!*

------*take her to the beach and let her dig to her heart's content*

May 24

I've learned a great trick of luring Della outside or into the kitchen where she sleeps or stays during our absence. She has taken delight of exploring through the house and would not come when we call her. Tonight Steve had trouble calling Della down from upstairs. I reassured him that I'd fix it. So I went to the pantry between the side door and the kitchen and alerted Della to the sound she had become so attracted to - the shaking of the dog food container. Yes, Della ran down in a heartbeat.

2 Likes, 0 Comments

May 25

Photo taken and captioned by Jana of Happy Tails:

"I am pretty sure those two are liquored up."

Della???

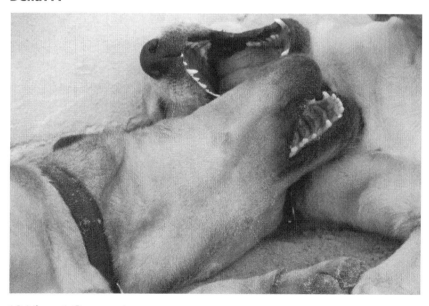

18 Likes, 1 Comment

------*LOLest!!*

May 25

Della's lump has significantly reduced, thanks to the antibiotics. But she still has to take those pills for ten more days and hasn't had any side effects so far. And she's ready to hit the big ONE in two days!

6 Likes, 3 Comments

------*Happy Birthday Della!!*

------*Take care of her!*

------*6 more years and she will settle down.*

May 26

We had dinner on the patio with the neighbors Jean and Jeff while their dog Lily ran around with our Della. Here we were, relaxing in our nice casual clothes, sitting comfortably, and enjoying our cocktails. It was a beautiful night with the salmon grilling nearby. Then it turned chaotic with Lily stamping her paw on Steve's light-colored shorts and Della stamping hers on Jean's white shirt. They had just gotten out of the fishpond and rolled around in the dirt. Our clean casual clothes became dirty dog clothes. And our dinner was constantly interrupted by the dogs' rackets such as Lily rummaging through the ice bucket and Della nudging our legs in demand to throw the ball. Geez, we felt like new parents with newborns but it sure was fun!

7 Likes, 1 Comment

------*You need to have a reality TV show all about Della!!! :)*

May 26

Della's birthday present from Jean and Jeff...
Completely destroyed in two hours.

5 Likes, 0 Comments

May 26

A year ago just now an unnamed puppy, the size of a Nerf ball,
laid waiting inside her mommy, eyes shut and curled-up along
with her ten siblings. Waiting and waiting to be born into this
dog-loving world...

18 Likes, 3 Comments

------It was a win-win!!!! :)

------(From Nora the breeder) Happy Birthday Della!!!! It was a memorial!

------Not sure who is luckier...you guys or Della! Love her adventures!

May 27

Happy Birthday, Della! Here comes your ice cream!

56 Likes, 15 Comments

------*Happy Birthday Della. Is that a Frosty Paw ice cream treat?*

------*(Bainy replies) No, REAL ice cream!*

------*She appears to be waiting SO patiently! Amazing!*

(All the rest of comments say "Happy Birthday, Della!")

May 27

Yum yum...

21 Likes, 4 Comments

------*cute...it's her birthday, right???*

------*(Bainy replies) Yes, she turns one today!*

------*Now you'll have to be on guard for the "terrible twos"....*

------*Please tell me she didn't eat the candle!*

May 28

Happy Memorial Day from Sandbridge...Della got another birthday treat: her first serious swim in the ocean. Last summer she was too little to go beyond the shore and the waves were too big for her. But now Della actually hits the waves, not afraid of how big they are. And she knows better than to go under so she just jumps right over the waves to catch her orange tube toy. Her coat, long stiff from grass and dirt, is now much softer from an ocean bath!

9 Likes, 0 Comments

May 28

Della got nipped on the nose by a gigantic sand crab but hasn't learned. She still goes after them...

3 Likes, 2 Comments

------☹

------*But they are so irresistible!*

May 29

(Steve and I are spending a week at my parents' beach cottage, along with Della)

Flies are just terrible here at Sandbridge since there is hardly any breeze. During our long walk up to the Dam Neck Lodge, Della had a hard time keeping those flies away, trying to swat them with her big paw and even bite them. That's why we encouraged Della to jump into the ocean which she did several times. She's now

napping peacefully inside the cottage, her paws occasionally twitching. I'm sure she is dreaming about swatting flies.

3 Likes, 2 Comments

------(From Elizabeth who just moved to Malibu) So many times I've heard people from the west coast say they don't like the east coast, because there are so many bugs. I never liked those pesky biting flies that show up when there is a land breeze or no breeze like you mentioned, but let me tell you the bugs are every bit as bad on the west coast. We went to the beach on Sunday and swarming the sand were what I believed to be sand fleas. I've never seen them before, but when you put your foot down a cloud of these bugs jumped and landed back down on the sand. There are also gnats everywhere all of the time. I've been told I can expect horseflies and mosquitoes to emerge soon, too. So, I feel your pain!

------One reason I think the Eastern Shore will never become a tourist mecca. Black flies. Greenhead flies. Mosquito birds.

May 29

Della just came out of the bathroom with Steve's toothbrush in her mouth, the bristle end unfortunately in. Uh, should we clean it thoroughly or just throw it away?

4 Likes, 14 Comments

------Toss it....definitely.

------toss it!!!

------just don't tell him...

------Brush her teeth. Silly dog. She's adorable.

------Won't matter of you don't tell him:)) Just kidding!!

------*Have you seen the places where Delta's mouth has been? I say, trash the brush and spring for another one.*

------*I'd keep it for her, as her new toothbrush and definitely buy Steve a new one.*

------*We all eat a peck of dirt. . .but maybe not the unmentionables dogs eat???*

------*Use it for her own toothbrush now. You do brush your dogs teeth right?*

------*Maybe she was asking to have help brushing her teeth!*

------*Don't tell him and put it back ha ha!*

------*Well she didn't throw it away because it had been in HIS mouth did she? I mean fair is fair! :)*

------*Aren't dog's mouths cleaner than people mouths? I read that somewhere.*

------*Run it through the dishwasher.*

------*One word - ick.*

May 30

So some of you say I can start using Della's stolen toothbrush to clean HER teeth? I cannot for one moment imagine myself doing that and I'm sure Della would have none of it. It'd be like trying to clean a running electric fan. But if her teeth look really bad or her breath cannot be helped by Altoids, then I will try. I see that in ten years.

2 Likes, 1 Comment

------*use PetSmart*

May 30

A whole day of rain is not good for a bored puppy. I thought five hours of Happy Tails would wear Della out but now we're back here at Sandbridge and she wants to get on the beach. Seems like a mini-hurricane out there.

5 Likes, 1 Comment

------*But Bainy, she's a water dog!!! How can you torture her so???? Joking of course!!! Good news, tomorrow is suppose to be sunny, no rain!!!*

May 30

Okay...got 47 more days before ending the book "Della on Facebook" on my birthday, after one full year of puppyhood for a 50-year-old woman hinged on estrogen decline. So far, over Della's 325 statuses with occasional pics have been posted along with your creative and empathetic comments. So please keep them coming!

10 Likes, 6 Comments

------*sure, but now it's time to get her own facebook thou. ;)*

------*Goodies! Looking forward to get that book.. :) Always enjoy reading what going on with Della these days. Love it when she gets in trouble... or do something funny..*

------*So for this birthday will you / Della get another puppy / sibling...then the posts can keep on going!!!!!*

------*Izzy's coming home from training soon so she will pick up the slack for Della.*

------*I will miss all the post. Keep them coming!*

------Della has been a joy for her audience, and obviously her courageous parents! Bravo, Bainy and Steve!

May 31

Della's new playmate

17 Likes, 2 Comments

------love that photo!

------Looks like it could be Della's little sister!

May 31

Lunch.

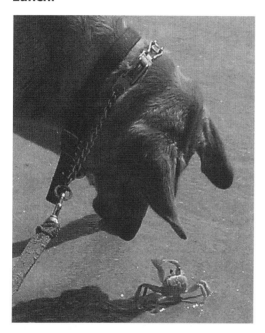

30 Likes, 10 Comments

------*Looks like the crab is on the defensive!..lol*

------*i wonder who will win??? Della is pretty intense about that crab...*

------*Ah did Della get pinched?*

------*Bainey, we had a yellow lab Kodi that would wander out in the sound to crab. He'd bring huge jimmies back to the pier and eat them up. It was always entertaining to watch. Every now and again a crab would fight back by latching onto those big lab lips, but they never really stood a chance. That Kodi was a champion crabber! Looks like Della wants that title now.*

------*Real good picture for your office*

------*Did that crab pinch Della's nose?*

June 1

Had a nice early morning walk on the beach. Uh, Della, I don't think it's a good idea to bury your nose into a sand crab's hole, especially big ones.

5 Likes, 1 Comment

------too funny

June 2

Okay, so we now know Della is an unfeared dog. Unlike our deceased Lab Olive, she does not cower, hide, or go into convulsion during fireworks or thunderstorms. Here at Sandbridge we had an overnight thunderstorm with intense lightnings and had to close all the windows and went back to sleep. Della did not even budge in her crate, only to look up and say "WTH?"

1 Like, 0 Comments

June 2

During our walk on the secluded beach between Sandbridge and Dam Neck, we came across a big red stingray stranded on the shore. It appeared to be suffocating so Steve used the sticks to nudge it back into the sea, cautious of its whiplike tail. Thank God we caught Della before she ran to the stingray. I don't want to imagine...

2 Likes, 0 Comments

June 3

Della resting after a morning swim

19 Likes, 5 Comments

------*The surf looks beautiful!!*

------*The pup looks exhausted!*

------*Wow it's a beautiful beachfront! Where's it? I'd love to go there and spend the night or two before heading to Florida one day soon and perhaps your Della and my Bella can be play dates ;)*

------*Is that your deck? Gorgeous!*

------*Love it!*

June 3

I just had a conversation with the mother of a six-year-old deaf girl. She wondered why her daughter spends so much time doting on her Pomeranian pooch, often ignoring hearing people around her. I explained the reason: It's because of communication. Deaf children and adults turn to their pets for companionship when they feel isolated from the majority world. They don't have to "talk" with their pets or try to understand communication. Therefore, deaf people can be the best pet owners. Admittedly, in the past when I became tired of missing out in group or family dinner conversation, I played with my dog. Sometimes I still do that, avoiding looking rude. Anyway, the mother was so relieved to know that her deaf daughter is not lonely after all with her dog. Della, you're ready to play???

28 Likes, 1 Comment

------*Thank you for sharing this post.*

June 4

It was the first guilty look we had seen on Della tonight as she hunched into the corner, ears limp and eyes downcast. The reason? She ate our small beet salads on the counter while we were out of the kitchen for a minute. Della tipped over the counter sideways and stole all of our fresh sliced cooked beets we had bought from the Sandbridge market yesterday. She even thought beets were delicious. But she feels downright guilty about eating some of our dinner. Once a dog looks contrite, it's forgiven.

7 Likes, 4 Comments

------This reminds me of the time our Bouvier, Louis, ate my mother's birthday pound cake (her favorite) which was cooling on the counter. He showed no signs of remorse, and I thought I'd misplaced the cake.

------Our childhood pet shaggy dog, Asta managed to eat an entire eye of the round roast that was on the counter, covered with foil without leaving any sign that it had been nabbed... until my mother lifted the foil to slice it.gone. not even a crumb. Asta had no remorse. gas. but no remorse.

------Sperry has mastered that "look"! I see it & think; uh oh & search the house! Generally I find the "hidden treasure" long after that look of contrition is gone!!! Haha!

------we always get a kick out of the "guilty look", but we have learned that it is just a look, Layla is not feeling guilty at all.

June 5

Here's an excerpt on my deceased dog Olive in my book "All Eyes, A Memoir of Deafness":

"One night, Steve and I took our yellow lab Olive for a walk, and our dog disappeared into the bushes yards away. After waiting, I wondered aloud if Olive had already done her business. Steve insisted that was what she was doing right at this moment. I stared at him doubtfully and asked, 'Well, then how do you know if you can't see Olive taking a poop fifty feet away in the total dark?' With a huge grin, he explained that once our dog's tags stopped jiggling and the leaves stopped rustling, it was happening right there. I tell you, hearing people's hearing never ceases to amaze me..."

It hasn't happened with Della yet but someday it will...Gotta turn up my hearing aid.

9 Likes, 5 Comments

------*Cute! lol Bainy My daughter (who is deaf) used to say I had "super-hero" ears and would vacillate between being impressed by it and frustrated at my ineptness when expecting me to hear something she could "see" a mile away... ;)*

------*Thanks for sharing...it's been years since I've heard leaves rustling and tags jingling. Wish more people were willing to be our "ears"*

------*Microwaving an 8 inch pizza, then open the door I HEAR the cheese popping. This is with my fabulous cochlear implant!!!!!!!!!!*

------*I had a blind friend who told me she could find her house if she got lost by listening for another house with windchimes. Depending on where the chimes were coming from, she knew which way to walk. I would never have thought of that.*

------*I love it*

June 5

Della nearly caused another scenario at Happy Tails and it was just fortunate timing for 27 other dogs to be distracted as they failed to notice her upcoming trick in that large indoors playpen. The staff there said she is the only dog that knows how to do it: Push up the latch and open the gate. But this time Della let only herself out, not 30 dogs as she did a while back. Good thing our garden gates have padlocks.

6 Likes, 5 Comments

------*This really makes me laugh!*

------my daughter used to do that in daycare and she would spring her brother out of his class too and the two would take off to entertain the seniors til they were caught!

------lol smart and mischief dog you got!

------She reminds me of a friend of mine who says, "I'm a bad influence on everyone I meet!"

------uh oh...my two dogs are there for next 10 days while we are renting at the beach. My sweet good dog, Roxie, won't break any rules but my young golden, Natty, might like to get into some trouble with Della!

June 6

When Della is in the house, she doesn't chew furniture, much less try to sit on them. That's good but I have to place each small wastebasket on the table - off the floor. Because every time Della passes a wastebasket, she would bury her head in there and pull out a wadded-up tissue or paper and chew it all over the floor. She has a thing for paper and once tore up the whole brand new box of Kleenex. That dog is a paper shredder.

5 Likes, 5 Comments

------I would love to have all my un-opened bills shredded by her! What's your address? :)

------Funny , but what a mess !!!!!!!!

------I don't know what it is with dogs and paper, esp soft papers....

------lol oh yes my Bella does that, too! lol paper shredder :) still its pain in the neck to pick them up, but better than picking up wood chips eh

------(From Nora the breeder) Her momma loved to shred newspaper Tiny little pieces all over the floor. She has grown out of that. Keep duck tape

out of her reach also, it was something about it she loved. Anything that was wrapped with duck tape she chewed to get the duck tape off. We finally figured that one out.

June 7

I look out the window and become envious of Della because she is lying on the straw bed and appearing so relaxed without a care in the world. No work, no emails, no deadlines, no casenotes, no schedules, no Internet or even this addictive Facebook...

6 Likes, 2 Comments

------I wish libby would stay outside by herself! We try and leave her out there and she acts like she's being tortured.

------Della has quite an eventful & hilarious FB history for being only a year old!!! :-)

June 7

It's summertime and the lightning bugs are back! Della is out there acting as if she needs to be institutionalized.

8 Likes, 2 Comments

------My dogs like to chase and eat June bugs. I am not sure I need to feed them dog food this time of year.

------lol funny!

June 8

Hosta Hardship inflicted by Della and her buddy Lily...

4 Likes, 10 Comments

------*The constant gardeners.*

------*Ew. One time while living in SB I went through the painstaking process of planting a hedge just inside our fence. I brought in soil, struggled to put down weed mat in the wind and put about 20 shrubs in the ground. The dogs were pleased with the new activity I provided them and promptly dug up each and every plant, shredded the weed mat and played in the soil.*

------*Awwwe naughty naught puppy dogs.*

------*huh you just let them running around and shredding them along your pedicured gardens without them being supervised? If so, no wonder! Lol*

------*oh no, not good.*

------*Is this your garden or do you sound so calm because it was at lily's house?*

------*heck they ll grow back again next year, right eh :) you just gotta love your dogs, no matter what ♥*

------*My Misty and her cousin Belle did the exact same thing. Hostas looked horrible all summer and didn't look good the next year. They were all spread out! Good luck!*

------*lol*

-------*holy cow......and I got all upset when mine just had holes punched in them from some hail.....*

June 10

We usually keep Della indoors on hot days but she likes to be out for a few hours especially in the shade. She knows how to make her own dirt bed on a day like this by going under the dense shrub, digging a wide shallow hole, and lying down in cool dirt. I'm sure Della will eventually dig deeper in July and August as our other dogs did. Olive once dug a three-foot-deep hole under the photinia and it was definitely air-conditioned down there.

2 Likes, 3 Comments

------*My dog has dug herself a very "nice" hole in my front yard.*

------*Chris' dog, Rivera, dug a hole to lie in the other day......and ended up in a biting ant colony.*

------*Ouch! I've been bitten by a single fire ant once in Florida and it hurt like hell!*

June 11

Unlike Jana the great photographer of Happy Tails, I can never take a good shot of Della and her playmate Lily together because they are like two flitting hummingbirds going in all directions. It's totally impossible despite my painstaking attempt to hand biscuits to both of these dogs over the gate at the same time in order to click a cute picture of their heads together. When one dog goes up, the other goes down. So I'm not going to waste any more time...

4 Likes, 1 Comment

------(From Jana of Happy Tails) Laughing......Bainy – happy to come over and show you my tricks. Oh yes...I have lots of tricks ☺.

June 12

Della??? What set you off at Happy Tails?

5 Likes, 14 Comments

------My goodness, that is quite the mixture of legs.

------Holy cow! Is she in Africa?

------Too bad she couldn't run in the Belmont, look at her go!

------"Wee I got me a new friend to chase after!"

------I looked really quick at this and thought it was a kangaroo!!

------she's airborne

------I'm betting on Della in the next Kentucky Derby!!!

------She levitates!

-----Did she learn the "crazies" from Desmond?

-----Somebody's got a really good camera!

------part kangaroo!

June 13

You can tell if the neighborhood dog Lily has already been brought in to play with Della early in the morning while you are still upstairs having coffee and reading the newspaper. How? Look at Della's muddy legs. So she and Lily have dove into the fishpond and then run around on the dirt. And Della hates to have her feet rinsed with the hose. Okay, if you want to stay dirty, you ain't coming inside.

2 Likes, 2 Comments

------is lily her BFF?

------(Bainy replies) Yes, she sure is.

June 13

Della, Della, Della...you need to stop all those dog escapades...

(Short Video of Della unlocking the gate and releasing the dogs at Happy Tails. She stands there with six or seven dogs in the enclosed pen. A few seconds later she stands up to the gate lock about four feet high, pulls the latch down with her paw, then pushes it up with her nose and finally pushes the gate open, releasing her buddies)

19 Likes, 12 Comments

------*Smart girl!!*

------*she is too smart for her own good!*

------*Uh-oh Bainy, That is one smart cookie-dog leading all those dogs astray. Too much fun!*

------*LOL hope she didn't get expelled!*

------*Did I see what I thought I saw? Della opened the gate and 'let the dogs out". Who let the dogs out? Woof! Clever girl!*

------*Looks like a scene from Marley and me--- too funny!*

June 13

I saw the video of Della's jailbreak on my cell phone, posted by Happy Tails, before picking her up. The staff there said she is now called "Houdini" because she does not unlock only the gates but also DOORS. Della would go through several rooms at this large daycare/boarding facility, pushing down the horizontal door handles, as she finds her way up to the front desk. Let's hope she does not eventually twist the round doorknob open with her mouth and that's the kind we have in our house...

13 Likes, 6 Comments

------OMG...I love these stories Bainy! But, i have to admit...i'm glad she's your dog and not mine..lol

------The really smart dogs are definitely challenging but so rewarding, too!

------I hope you are writing a book about Della's exploits...that dog is just too funny!!!!

------Sounds like you should train her for the agility trials or something. HOw cool is she?

------Bainy, It kind of reminded me of Jurassic Park where the residents learned their way around the park and how to escape!

------(From Jana the owner of Happy Tails) It reminds me that we need new LOCKS! :-)

June 14

OMG, that's even a better one. Della's done it again.

(New video posted by Jana of Happy Tails. She writes: "Della and the great escape! This is actually funny. We honestly could not figure out who was leaving the gate open and I was constantly on my staff 'CLOSE AND LOCK THE GATES!'")

(This second video of Della's release of the dogs is even better because someone behind the camera calls Della who is in the back of the dog crowd by the gate. She appears into scene and walks up and unlocks the gate and releases over 25 dogs, causing a huge stampede. Della is almost knocked over by the dogs behind her. All the dogs just run around the corner toward the pool. The mixture of laughter from the Happy Tails staff and barks are

heard in the video. This video would eventually become viral on YouTube.)

37 Likes, 23 Comments

------*Saw my Natty coming through the gate. I bet Della is his new hero.*

------*this is toooo funny*

------*Looks like time for the old chain and padlock ploy!*

------*She's watched the humans do it so she thought she would too! This is hilarious!*

------*She's watched the humans do it so she thought she would too! This is hilarious!*

------*Someone get that dog a suduko*

------*Doggie Breakout!*

------*Just like in the movies!*

------*Does Della have her own FB page yet? Fan club? Movie rights for sale? Book deal?*

------*This made my day! Thanks for sharing Della with us!*

------*Della has a human brain, smart dog!*

------*Della must have gotten her smarts from Bainy. Just joking, Steve.*

------*OMG..haha The great escape!!*

------*I AM GLAD SHE IS YOURS!*

------*I love it! Passed it around the Tides baseball game for everyone to watch :)*

------*I love all the dogs watching her...wonder how long it will be till they can ALL do it!*

June 14

Another video of Della's mischief...

(Jesse, one of the Happy Tails employees, took a brief video of Della at the gate from a distance while a few other dogs stood around. Della unlocked and opened the gate and some of the dogs were hesitant to escape while others just walked out casually. It was not really an escape as in the previous video but interesting to watch with Jesse's exasperated voice saying, "Della, Della, Della...")

12 Likes, 7 Comments

------*This cracks me up!*

------*Looks like where Fight Club was held*

------*So funny!!!*

------*Who wants to be in a stinkin cage. Not Della and most of her pals, but I did notice some were hesitant to leave....so funny and cute.*

------*Bainy, I changed my mind about bringing Sophie over for a play date with Della!:)*

------*She is one smart dog! We had Boomer - a golden retriever. He managed to make a hole in a two foot plaster wall. No pen could keep him - he either went over or under - concrete, finally, worked! He got written up in the paper and had the nickname, "King of Algonquin Park. Gorgeous, smart dog, but incorrigable!(Sp?)*

------*Notice how orderly and polite the others are.*

June 15

Hey, Della MAY be on the Channel 13 news at noon today so keep an eye out for it!

8 Likes, 7 Comments

------*Your beautiful smart baby is becoming infamous I think.*

------*I've heard she has a nose for news.*

------*You didn't take her to the zoo did you? "Yellow lab leads escape of lions, tigers, and bears.....oh my!"*

------*Oh my gosh! Let me know! I don't get that channel, but maybe it will end up on Youtube~!*

------*I'll watch for her.*

------*Just saw her!*

------*It was great fun to see her on the news!*

June 15

Della will be on Channel 3 at 6 PM with Barbara Ciara!

34 Likes, 15 Comments

------*Featuring Della, the escape artist!*

------*Bainy, I just saw the video of Della on 13 news! She's famous now!!!*

------*Just saw the clip from Happy Tails on channel 13. Fun!*

------*Awesome!! She must be Houdini's apprentice :)*

------*Spencer is jealous!!!! :)*

------*I wish I could watch the news in AZ, darn...Good luck, Della!*

------Bainey! Now everyone's going to find out about our little slice of doggie heaven.

------Sorry to miss it! Am working in the ED.

------(From Nora the breeder) Houdini Della! What a smart dog! I have saved it on DVR so I can show Burt! Her momma would be so proud!

------Saw it on the news this evening. Della, you are a celebrity for the doggie escapade.

------Our whole family laughed out loud.

------That is so awesome, Bainy. It's so nice to have news that makes you happy!

------(From one of Bainy's best friends who had missed it all) WHAT'S THE OCCASION?

June 15

(With the news coverage link)

Okay, here's the news coverage...(sorry, no captioning for the deaf but I'll explain everything briefly) Jana first tells about the mystery of dogs running loose into the front office. She first blames her employees, threatening to fire them. Next, she explains how Della unlocks the gate. Finally, in the end she declares she's going to get better locks! Poor Cliff says he and other workers had to defend themselves. He shrugs and jokingly says it was all his fault for leaving the gate open. Then you see what the little dog says. So Della really did it!

38 Likes, 32 Comments

------Whoooo let the dogs out!!?!!?!! Haha!

------Just saw it...LOL!

-----*Very cool! I noticed you must of pleaded the 5th or said "no comment" when picking up the devious Della while TV cameras were rolling.....LOL*

------*She would've made a great service dog for someone with physical challenges :)*

------*She's a star!!! You look terrific on camera too Bainy!*

------*I watched it live!! We had to put our husky down a couple of weeks ago. Wahoo Wali Crenshaw the chocolate lab needs a new friend...does Della have cousins???*

------*Oh Bainy!! what a great story!! And wonderful free publicity for Happy Tails...My max's favorite beauty parlor!!*

------*Della is a whiz kid! What a fun story!*

------*Della looked like a professional. What a smart doggy.....*

------*You (and Della) look great. My boys got quite a kick out of this!!! Thanks for sharing*

------*It was really a fun spot!*

------*That is the best jail-break ever!*

------*It was great. I saw coverage on both TV stations- WTKR was the best.*

------*Della, the TV star!*

------*An agent, newsletter and blog site next! What a great clip! Wonderful change from routine news!!*

------*Bainy- I thought you were supposed to help people get AND KEEP their jobs, not have your dog sabotage someone's job. LOL I miss seeing you. We should grab a coffee sometime soon.*

------*Adorable...saw it on the news in Roanoke!!!*

June 16

Della has been acting like a spoiled celebrity here at home so I'm going to put her to work. She was just offered a position as a watch dog at the Mecklenburg Correctional Center and will start on Monday...No, just kidding.

10 Likes, 8 Comments

------*can I get her autograph?*

------*How are you handling the paparazzi?*

------*(Bainy replies) Hmm, Dana, you got me thinking...I'll decline the Mecklenburg offer and have Della work as an attack dog for the paparazzi...*

------*Bailiff would be so proud.*

------*I loved Della's story on the news...that was so funny!*

------*Too funny!*

------*I bet the inmates were behind the Della-Mecklenburg initiative....*

------*A correctional facility!!! She'd figure out how to work the locks and let everyone out.*

June 16

30 more days before ending the book "Della on Facebook". Do you think I can still survive my entire 50th year by then? I don't think a puppy and a middle-aged woman together have been so bad...

4 Likes, 4 Comments

------*She has kept you young!*

------*Please don't stop posting about Della.*

------*Everyone loves Della and you, too! Please don't stop!*

------do you start the sequel then? "della's new sibling"

June 17

Wow...the number of viewers have jumped up to over 2500 for "Della the Yellow Lab Causing A Jailbreak!" on YouTube. One asked if she was in Seattle. Good Job, Jana!

8 Likes, 2 Comments

------You just wait - this video will be going "viral" and she'll be on the Today Show!

------(From Jana of Happy Tails) NO! NO! NO! The local news killed me. :-)

June 17

Della had her much-deserved treat after all the hoopla over the weekend: A swim in the Chesapeake Bay. Her coat was stiff with dirt and grass, although she looked clean from the outside. So Della was taken to First Landing Beach and chased her orange tube toy into the rough waves. And got a good scrub in the salt water and came out much softer and silkier. Worked better than her despised water hose.

4 Likes, 0 Comments

June 18

The security at Happy Tails has increased to a maximum level in order to prevent any more major escapes intentionally caused by Della. Yes, the locks have been changed.

13 Likes, 6 Comments

------She will think of something else!!! ;))

------Have they upped the charges...especially yours? HA! the whole thing is just too funny.

------Della will figure an escape somehow. Our first dog used to climb over chain link fences!

------now we all can take our dogs to a maximum security lock up! I feel so much better

------Dogs will be dogs!!! They are smarter than we know. Della will figure out another escape route. :-)0

------A celebrity and a convict at the same time! Della is in good company! I believe there are a bunch of celebrities in the same situation. At least Della gets to come home at night!!

June 18

As luck would have it, I caught Della before she ate another big can of fish food. Why can't I leave any food unattended on the patio table just for a single second?

2 Likes, 5 Comments

------Because you have a dog!

------That stuff has a rather irresistible smell to dogs.

------You can train her to leave it and people food alone

------Izzy stole a hamburger from Cindy's plate this evening. It's not just Della.

------hope that wasn't ur supper....that would really stink.....on three counts.

June 20

It's going to be hot in the next few days and I'm going to find Della doggie ice cream.

5 Likes, 6 Comments

------Frosty Paws!!!

------She whispered in my ear that she would be fine with Human Ice Cream if you can't find the doggie kind:)

------ice cream no sugar in store would be fine

------Skinny Dip frozen yogurt has pre-packed doggy dips. It's $1/bowl. You can also get regular and PB Frosty Paws at Harris Teeter.

------do stores sell ice cream for cats ,too?

------(Bainy replies) I don't know, Sharon. They ought to make fish ice cream for cats...

June 20

Wait until Della comes home from VERY Happy Tails...

16 Likes, 7 Comments

------I hope you bought more than 1 box. It's going to be a hot summer!

------Bainy, where did you buy those? The commissary stopped selling them and Zeus loves them!

------Zoey loves Frosty Paws!

------(Bainy replies) @Kirk: They are in the frozen treat section in the ice cream aisle at the Marketplace on 21st Street.

-----(Kirk comments) Perfect! On my way now...

------Didn't agree with our dog's Tummy. Tried before. I am sure She will be Fine!!! Enjoy!!!

------We had bacon flavored frosty paws in the refrigerator once and I ate one not knowing it was frozen grease masquerading in kind and in price as dog ice cream... I'll never go back now to the real thing.

June 20

Blue Bunny and other ice cream companies: You should start selling Frosty Paws from your ding-dong trucks. Dogs will have a good reason to chase them - in a nice way.

11 Likes, 1 Comment

------What a good idea!!!

June 23

Oh dear, after all the rain, Della and her buddy Lily are muddying up themselves...

2 Likes, 0 Comments

June 24

I'm having a girls' dinner party to welcome back the Norfolk native Elizabeth Cope from California and had to clean up muddy Della and even her collar which is once again bright red. Never have a dirty dog when you have company...

8 Likes, 0 Comments

June 24

You know we all see a pro basketball player like Michael Jordan making a slam dunk by turning his body sideways in midair and aiming for the net. Well, that's what Della does when she aims for food. While we cleaned up after my dinner party for a friend, Della was finally let in and ran to the dining table, elevated, turned sideways in midair, and stole a dinner roll in one swipe, all in her mouth.

11 Likes, 6 Comments

------*I love your dog!*

------*LOL!!! I love it! Della Jordan!*

------*Dont let her watch Michael Jordan anymore then!*

------*A real athlete!*

------*The rolls were very good and moist. Too bad hers was not warm like mine.*

------*I think she embodies the Nike slogan: just do it!*

June 25

Della, Della, Della, please don't pluck another one of those poor goldfishes from the garden pond and leave it for dead on the patio. They are my pets, too...

7 Likes, 4 Comments

------*:(poor fishy.....*

------*We had a puppy come over and gave our fish a workout! But they survived.*

------*We had to fence off the pond so the dogs couldn't get to the fish.*

------*You may be able to put a metal grate over the pond so there is less room for a dog snout to go in.*

June 26

About a week after I got Della for my birthday last July, I met Matt Myrick whose booth was next to mine at the Richmond conference and showed him pictures of Della. Having grown up with large dogs, Matt expressed interest in getting a Lab puppy for his wife but did not feel totally ready at the time. But I urged him to drive to Della's birthplace an hour away and take a look at the remaining litter. Boy, I really persuaded Matt to the point where I actually ushered him out of the exhibit room. We are again across from each other at this Charlottesville conference and he said he would never trade Della's sister for anything!

17 Likes, 2 Comments

------*that's cute*

------*(From Nora the breeder) I am so happy! Both of the best puppy owners ever!*

June 27

We've had a scary moment with Della today and learned a lesson: Even if you leave a full bowl of fresh water outside, your dog can still get dehydrated. Della has run so much at the Meadowbrook park and with Lily the neighbor that she has neglected to drink out of that big bowl we left by the door. She was sluggish when I got home from the conference trip and couldn't even lift herself up from the flower bed. Of course, I started giving her plenty of water inside the house as well as fed her well. At least she has not thrown up. Dehydration can be a serious situation with dogs because they don't always drink from the bowl you leave for them. And the Internet says it's better for you to give your dehydrated dog Gatorade than plain water for survival because it contains electrolytes which water does not have. Electrolytes, not only water, can save lives.

5 Likes, 6 Comments

------*You're a good momma, Bainy. And I remember when you were just a little toddler.*

------*I have six bowls for mine and they drink from just two at different times.*

------*I called animal control on someone today for leaving a dog in a pen with no water. It's only about the fifth time I have called! Glad your pup is okay!*

------*hey Bainey....leaving water is all u can do. Reminds me of a lesson I learned, when I was volunteer fire fighting, when people would call about cats in trees..."Ain't never found a cat's bones in a tree." Della woulda 'figured it out...ps..luv ur luv!*

------*oh my goodness, keep her cool and thanks for the tip about Gatorade, I shall buy some for in case of emergency to store for this summer.*

------I wonder, if a dog is lethargic but conscious, if using a turkey baster full of water and gatorade and dribbling into their mouths is the way to help them quickly. (Kinda of like a giant eyedropper.)

June 28

Della is back to her old self after being dehydrated yesterday. Her back leg is no longer cramping. For dogs there are definitely visible signs of dehydration such as lethargy and temporary paralysis of back legs. From now on we'll give Della some Gatorade if she doesn't bother to drink water when she should. In the next several days she will have to be kept indoors most of the time because of the heat wave. Oh boy, she's going to be destructive as ever...

2 Likes, 2 Comments

------Is it really okay to give them some Gatorade?

------(Bainy replies) Yes, according to several websites

June 28

Della is no Serena Williams or Michael Jordan because she doesn't like Gatorade. So I will have to use chicken broth mixed with water the next time she gets dehydrated. Besides, Della is doing much better. Back to Happy Tails tomorrow.

2 Likes, 10 Comments

------Water it down some, Bainy. A trainer at Hickory once told me it's too concentrated directly out of the bottle. That's why I always buy the powder & mix my own. My kids wouldn't drink it straight if they had to now. They water it down some...

------*(Bainy comments)* I just did - 1/3 broth and 2/3 water. Della drank it as if it was an ice cold beer.

------*(Same friend replies)* I was talking about the Gatorade! Haha! I followed your advice & gave Sperry some this morning with her breakfast & more at lunch! She's been more of a "water is a toy" vs. "oh! I should drink this" kind of puppy!!! Don't get me started on how she goes psycho over the hose & water when I'm watering plants! It's a professional sport to her! She jumps like Air Jordan to get that stream!!! :-)

------*You can purchase electrolyte powder from Southern States, then just mix in the food - I use it for the horses before and after extreme rides or in heat waves.*

------*My girls don't like it either but they do like bouillon and rice. I do it very soupy at first and if they hold it down I gradually add rice, then chicken and then I might add some pumpkin (NOT pumpkin pie --just plain pumpkin is easy on their digestion)*

------*I've been warned by our vet anything with salt/sugar is hard on their kidneys :/*

------*I'd also worry about the salt content. You can make it yourself with chicken bones!!!*

------*The vet told us to boil chicken in plain water (if not boneless remove bones and if desired, skin) then to add some white rice and serve at a "soupy" consistency.*

------**Remove the bones 'when done' if not boneless*

------*hahaha! I meant that! :)*

June 29

Wow...Della's jailbreak video on YouTube has become much more viral in the past two days, jumping up to almost 5000 views. Interesting about the sudden increase...

7 Likes, 6 Comments

------What is the link for that tube, pls?

------I told you so! You will be making the tv show rounds.....the today show, good morning america, letterman........Della's a STAR!

------(Bainy replies with a pasted YouTube link)

------Do you get paid for each view?

------(Bainy replies) No – I have no idea how it works. I am okay with the "free video"!

------I wish I could get Della's theme song "Who Let the Dogs Out?" out of my head now! ;)

June 30

I don't normally put Della in daycare on a Saturday but today is so hot that I just took her to the Happy Tails pool or she will drive us crazy in the house all day. So you all stay cool and drink plenty of water!

7 Likes, 2 Comments

------I just took Sophie for a swim in the river...bath, and now napping next to me on couch!

------you are such a great mom to Della. She is so lucky to have you, Bainy.

July 1

Oh great...I forgot how much Labs shed during the heat of summer. I'd need to buy a high-powered vacuum cleaner and lint brushes. Della was up in our bedroom stretching after a brief morning nap and shaking herself awake, releasing a million tiny yellow hair strands illuminated by the sun ray through the window. It was like watching confetti fluttering around and then raining down at the Times Square on New Year's Eve. Swell...

6 Likes, 5 Comments

------*Imagine having two border collie/husky doggies during the heat!!!! I suffer!!!!*

------*We call wrigley pigpen from the peanuts because she looks like she has a cloud of dust following her from all this shedding!*

------*Bainy...we buzzed our 4 year old lab's coat for the first time this summer.....she loves it!*

------*Having a lab mix and a golden retriever, I swear by the Dyson animal vacuum cleaner...*

------*Combine it with the dirt bath mine likes to take....fun fun*

July 1

Feeding Della ice cubes on this hot day. She's eating them like popcorn.

5 Likes, 0 Comments

July 1

It's hard to believe that I have only 15 more days to finish the book "Della on Facebook". As some of you may not know, that would mark a full year of puppyhood for a 50-year-old woman. So far, there have been 387 posts/photos about Della. I have decided to self-publish the book and am now working on the cover. And will need to ask the FB headquarters for permission to use its name for the title. Hopefully, "Della on Facebook" will go into print and Kindle by next spring or sooner. I would like to thank Jana Underwood of Happy Tails for all her great photos as well as all the fun Della has had there!

25 Likes, 2 Comments

------*I can't wait to read it!*

------*Ok. Now it makes sense. A book. I was wondering why you posted so much about Della. I mean she is cute and all but I was kind of worried. Good to know there was a reason that didn't involve fanaticism about your dog. She is cute. We have a black lab. He is sit com some days. Ti is crazy living with a lab. Yup, sheds all the time. And yes, I do very little on Facebook so I am way behind the curve.*

July 3

It sure is nice not to have been seen for five hours and become sorely missed - and someone stands up, almost as tall as I am, and grasps my shoulders with those big hands and says, "So, how was your day?" It was Della.

7 Likes, 1 Comment

------*Mine jumps on my chest OW! Lol, I'm tall and you're a cute petite.* ☺

July 4

Steve and I went to get ice cream after dinner and took Della along with us. We each ordered a different flavor in one big scoop: Butter Pecan for Steve, Milky Way for me, and Vanilla for Della. We were one happy family on a hot night!

13 Likes, 1 Comment

------Nothing like ice cream for humans or dogs!

July 4

Homemade popsicle for Della.
Recipe: Fill the plastic container with 2/3 water, 1/3 unsalted chicken broth, and a few kibbles. Freeze it overnight.

22 Likes, 8 Comments

------*Bainy that looks delicious. I hope the afterlife brings me back as one of your dogs...happy 4th.*

------*refreshing!*

------*Does it give her brain freeze?*

------*thanks for the recipe, I shall make some for my dogs.*

------*Brilliant!! How do you keep her confined so she doesn't bring it all over the house? And if you put her outside it's gonna melt. I think Max would love this though....he comes a running every time he hears the ice maker!!*

------*(Bainy replies) I left the popsicle inside at first but then took it outside when it was melting. Della went crazy over it!*

------*Great idea!!!!!!*

------*Pure Heaven!*

July 5

I need your opinion on heartworm pills. For years we gave our dogs the brand Heartgard without any problem. But then for some reason the vet no longer sells Heartgard and first recommended Interceptor for Della and she had no problem with this brand. And then Interceptor went out of supply nationwide due to lack of plant nutrients. So the vet had to switch to Triflexis and warned that it would cause nausea unless I gave it to Della along with her meal. She threw up despite her full stomach and that happened twice, first last month and again this month. I'm not keen on Triflexis which has flea control as well. I want to go back to Heartgard and found that I can order it on PetMed.com but don't know if the vet would approve. Any ideas?

0 Likes, 28 Comments (I'm including all of these opinions here so you can learn)

------*My vet gave me the option to order Heartgard online but I am now trying a new one that is equal to Heartgard and it is called Iverhart Max. My dog too threw up after taking Interceptor and was also told that Heartgard is no longer in the vet office. Hope this helps.*

------*Libby is on Iverheart.*

------*I am now having trouble to order Sentential, then need to use heart guard for both dogs. I do worry about several other products, too.*

------*We've been using Advantage Multi for about 18 months. Nothing to swallow, I just apply it to the back of Zeus' neck once a month.*

------*We use the topical one that is for fleas, ticks and heartworm. Of course I can't remember the name right now....*

------*use advantage which you apply to neck of animal*

------*I gave Trifexis to both of my dogs for the first time last month. One of my dogs got a bad reaction to it -- fever, very lethargic, wouldn't eat, etc. My other dog threw up after taking the pill. They were on Interceptor but can't get that any more. I don't know what other heart prevention medication is available. As an FYI, Costco now carries Pet Meds for much less...I'll pass on any helpful info that my vet provides...Let us know what you find out too, Bainy.*

------*(Bainy replies) Thanks to you all for your suggestions. I really think Heartgard would be the way to do it and I can also still use Advantage II for flea control.*

------*Meagan has been on the Triflexis about a year.....she hasn't seem to have any problems.*

------*hi cousin. Hutch too has been on trifexis for almost a year. each dose lasts a month and with the 1st 2 doses he did get sick but after that they adjust and it usually gets better. it works great for us out here in flea, tick, mosquito country! he hated the topkcal kind and would run and hide from us when trying to apply plus he loves getting wet, so the trifexis works great for us. u may just need to give it time for her to adjust..good luck!*

------But it doesn't work for ticks. That's a pain.

------Not sure which one you are talking about but i know the Trifexis works great for ticks :)

------Call around to other vets for the Interceptor

------I've been using Iverhart also for more than a year now with no problems for either of my dogs. I only switched because Heartgard just kept going up in price. Extra bonus is $3 rebate with Iverhart.

------I just started using Triflexis without any problems except an increase in itching for the dogs, along with more shedding than usual for my 13 year old dog, but no nausea.

------Interesting, i was told I'd have to use some addition to prevent ticks. I thought trifexis took care of 3 things--heartworms, intestinal worms and fleas.

------I use heartgard no problems and the sell it at Costco now....

------I have always used Interceptor as it is believed to be the safest on the market, and I have always ordered it from Petmeds (except when I was able to get it from the SNIP van in VA). No vet has ever had a problem with my doing so. Although heart worm meds are absolutely necessary in many parts of the country, (I have not needed to use them in the last two places I've lived :)), they are believed to have long term negative effects in dogs. Bundling them with flea/tick prevention can make them even more hard on the body.

------@ Mary, that is strange, it must work b/c we have had 0 ticks and that is the only prevention he is on & we live in TICK country out here on

the Eastern Shore of VA. They leave him alone 100% so hopefully it will work for you dog. My dog is a lab and about 96 lbs. The vet says it covers fleas, ticks, mosquitoes & heartworm :)

-----(Mary replies) My dog hasn't gotten one yet either but I keep thinking he will. If you read the trifexiis package, it doesn't mention ticks.

------Yes, u can get them from 800petmeds.com , if they need prescription from the vet, your vet have to give it to them by faxing, and your vet can not refuse as you have right to choose different pharmacy, I have been ordering with them for years, it saves hundred bucks...

------Get a prescription for heartgard and call 1800pet meds

------Calvin's on Trifexis and sometimes he vomits after taking them and I've noticed that he seems to scratch alot for about a week after taking it. My personal favorite was the Interceptor.

------I give Heartgard to my aussie for a long time .. she is doing good with heartgard

------Think we are giving Zelle Sentinel..never thought of questioning it..should I?

------Sentinel is what I give my dogs...but the plant got closed down because of the human drugs it was producing...saying a few months that it will be closed down but that has been 7 months ago. My vet is selling Triflexis but not really wanting to go to it but might. I am almost half tempted to go with Heartgard and get the vet to write a prescription for my dogs and order it online or have the vet special order it for me. The Triflexis is twice as much as the Sentinel. I have one more month worth of doses for my dogs so holding out before changing. My vet did say the dogs could have problems with it for the first month or so...really don't like changing meds with my dogs!

------HeartGuard doesn't protect against whipworms.. common in our area. Due to medicine allergies, when Interceptor became unavailable while the *company redoes their production plant we switched Sasha over to REVOLUTION. It's topical, does heartworm, whipworms, fleas & ticks. It's a little pricey, but through online at Drs foster & Smith, it isn't much more than interceptor + the flea/tick stuff we were using. It dries fast & she can get in the water within a very short period of time. We won't be switching back to interceptor... Revolution is so much easier!*

------Use Comfortis for fleas in summer season only. Fleas fall off within the hour. Know that will have to change when we have a real emergency!!

July 8

Della has been sniffing around my legs since I arrived home from a weekend trip. I guess she detects something I got at the airports in Hartford and Philly. Maybe I'll put her to work as a bomb sniffer.

4 Likes, 3 Comments

------At least you know you're bomb-free, nobody slipped one into your handbag.

------MAKE HER EARN ALL THOSE ICE CREAM TREATS YOU MAKE HER! LOL

------Give her the training. She could make a ton of money and you and Steve could retire early.

July 9

While I was away for the weekend, Steve took Della out for a ride one hot night, stopped at a place, tied her to a parking meter, went inside, and kept an eye on her through the window. Della just sat behaviorally and watched at people walking by, not even

trying to pull away from the meter. She knew. Steve came out with her favorite summer treat: Vanilla ice cream.

19 Likes, 2 Comments

------Aw really she behaved that well, are you kidding me since she broke out of 'jail' at the daycare!? Lol ;) Bet it was the smell of MOO that she knew Steve would give her a scoop!

------glad nobody nabbed her!

July 9

Cliff at Happy Tails told me that Della would not eat her lunch I brought in a zip-lock bag. That happened only today. I asked why. Cliff said it was because Della was afraid she wouldn't be allowed back in the pool if she ate. She probably knows one of the summer rules: Never go swimming after you eat...

4 Likes, 4 Comments

------she's obeying mom's rules!

------oh c'mon, really!?

------Mom's rules..gotta wait an hour.

------Lunch! Don't tell Calvin. Cuz he only gets breakfast and dinner.

July 10

As much as she hates going to the vet, Della tried to act like a Houdini again by going up to two doors in the examination room and had no luck with the vertical and round doorknobs. So Friendship Veterinary Hospital is unescapable. The good news is

that Della's heartworm test is negative and the vet agreed on Heartgard which is back in stock.

7 Likes, 0 Comments

July 11

Afternoon Treat

8 Likes, 3 Comments

------*What a great mom!*

------*Frosty Paws?*

------*(Bainy replies) Yes. Peanut butter flavored.*

July 11

A fourteen-month-old puppy is a very long way, I mean painfully away, from adulthood. Della just dragged a 3' x 5' hall rug into her open 2' x 3' grate to chew on. But that was not all. She also nearly ate a rubber doormat decorated with wine bottles. I mean, a doormat and a rug on the same day...What the heck is going on?

2 Likes, 9 Comments

------*yeah long way to settle down she still is a puppy...*

------*Have you tried giving her a Nylabone? Sounds like a bit of anxiety.*

------*(Bainy replies) Della is now sound asleep on her bed. She still has her Nylabone nearby. Maybe she had one of her mini-breakdowns.*

------*I hold Scoobys for him sometimes. :)*

------*Terrible Twos!*

------*Good grief Bainy she's a puppy. Similar is going on here and my puppy is almost 4 lol*

------*I'm dog sitting a 4 y/o mutt who has not yet calmed down at day 3. She has already figured out how to jump the fence to look in the driveway for her overdoting mommy. Thank god she does not run off. 7 more days to go.............OMG*

------*Bainy, I already see what you mean. The puppies don't get better, they just get bigger and therefore can think of and do a lot more damage!!! Sophie also loves to chew up our doormats and bathroom mats, in addition to shoes, eyeglasses, pens, and anything she can reach which is a lot more now that she can stand and see the countertops!!!*

------*Teething is possible. Up to age 2 yrs. Desi did this until that age. I have had shoes, eyeglass frames and leather purse chewed up. Also cardboard boxes.*

July 12

Every time we let Della loose in the house, the first thing she does is go into the dining room and steal one of the homegrown tomatoes left on the windowsill to ripen. I just caught her with one as big as a baseball in her mouth, luckily before she pierced the tomato with her fangs. I'd prefer that Della eat a baseball instead of a tomato we have tried hard to grow with tender loving care...

2 Likes, 6 Comments

------*Try to figure out what draws her to that and get something similar.*

------*My girls like to eat fresh fruit and veg. I don't think eating only processed dog food can be good. Maybe she's trying to tell you something.*

------*My Mickey used to take the pumpkins out of the garden, right when were ready to pick them! He really like the taste of them.*

------*Della seems like a challenge!*

------*Find some other stuff she likes to eat and put in the window sill:) Put the tomatoes on top of the refrigerator;)*

------*I love Della and I haven't even met her. Love reading about her. She's a real character - just like her mom!*

July 12

I think I'm going to get a patent for homemade doggie popsicles and name them Chicksicles.

3 Likes, 2 Comments

------*Dellasicles*

------*What about pupsicles?*

July 13

Do you think we need a bigger chair?

19 Likes, 12 Comments

------*Yes.*

------*Hahahaha!*

------*She's beggin' u to go shopping!*

------*A whole lot bigger- yes! Like a love seat.*

------*or maybe put Della on a diet*

------*I think Della needs a bigger chair-not you.*

------*I've got the perfect chair(s)!!!*

July 14

Here I was sleeping heavily in the middle of my colorful dreams and then POOF! Della, all 75 pounds of her, had jumped on my bed, licked my ears, walked over me, and danced around me, her tail whipping my face. Good thing today is only Saturday...

13 Likes, 3 Comments

------*Sunday, too!! ;)*

------*My gift from Della would be bruises!*

------*40 lbs of Izzy landed on me at 1 AM. Must have been something in the air.*

July 14

Finally a good "Sit still" picture of Della and her best buddy Lily. Good Job, Jean Swartz!

25 Likes, 7 Comments

------That is precious!

------they are both smiling!

------Thanks for sharing. This pic made me laugh. It's perfect.

------finally! heh so cute! :)

------I just saw a dog across the street from your parent's old house that looks exactly like Della! Is she visiting downtown???

------That is so cute!

------Aww that's an awesome pic! Cute!

July 15

During a visit with my parents today I reminded them that it has been exactly a year since I got the pint-sized Della. Mom said, "Oh? Is she a horse by now?" Uh, no, not that big...

5 Likes, 2 Comments

------Happy Birthday, Bainy!

------Happy Birthday Cuz! Luv your Della stories...

July 16

Thank you all for my birthday wishes...It really made my day! I can't believe it's been exactly one year since I got Della and yes, this is the end of "Della on Facebook". Don't worry, I will definitely keep posting on Della as many of you have requested — just for fun, not another book! In fact, Della has given me the best 50th year, never mind the unpredictable hormones or graying hair. Undoubtedly I feel much younger than ever. Owning a puppy, albeit the mischievous one, is actually beneficial for a middle-aged woman. Combined with laughter, a new pet is the best medicine. Thank you, Steve, for the best birthday gift, and no, I don't need another puppy this time. And thank you, Della, for making my birthday several years younger...and it's time to stamp your paw on the last page of "Della on Facebook" and bark in gratitude to your Facebook friends. Again, thank you all for your support! OX

To see Della in action, go to YouTube and type:

"Della the Yellow Lab Causing a Jailbreak!"

Made in the USA
Charleston, SC
14 September 2012